INNERMORE

INNERMORE

SEEING WHAT LIES WITHIN

MICHAEL JANES

ISBN: 979-8-9885070-1-7 (Paperback)
ISBN: 979-8-9885070-0-0 (eBook)

Library of Congress Control Number: TXu 2-377-389

Any references to historical events, real people, or real places are used fictitiously. Names, characters, and places are products of the author's imagination.

Book design by Glen Edelstein, Hudson Valley Book Design

Printed by IngramSpark, in the United States of America.

First printing edition 2023.

Dedicated to: My loving partner Cindy.
The LA Woman in my life!
And
Henry B. who helped me become
the writer I am today.

BOOK 1
CONFUSION

Your life is not about the story.
Your life is a journey.

CHAPTER 1

RIGHT FROM
THE START

I FIND IT DIFFICULT to write about the past. So much of my life has been unpleasant. When I write about the past, the walls of denial come down. My well-established coping mechanism gets put on hold so I can see what's inside. It's painful then to decide what to write.

At some point, the pain becomes great enough so that the form I make myself out to be is resurrected, and I stop writing. A spurt of so-called "reality" is whisked away as I escape to a more familiar place. Writing can be like this at times. In fact, life can be like this for me.

I spend my days keeping the boss happy, keeping this body healthy, and keeping the bill collectors at bay, but I'm often not up to the task. It's not a good idea to just call in sick whenever Monday rolls around, though.

Love won't be found if I don't have the will for it. The train won't be caught unless I make a run for it. The cold will be cold unless I choose to dress for it.

If life just followed my rules, then everything would be okay, but this is not the way it works. I either learn about life, or I put on my game face, and up come the walls.

As a child, I decided that this was how it would be. Back then, I was G.I. Joe, I was an airplane designer, or maybe I was a rock star on a particular night. As long as I kept my door closed and no one came in, I was fine. Someone always came in, though.

I blamed the fear, sadness, and confusion that I lived with on my family. There was plenty that one could point to there. However, things didn't always add up. The dysfunctionality of my family couldn't explain enough of me. My unhappiness would often eclipse the events that surrounded me. I believed there was more to what was going on, and this created a dilemma.

I felt something, but didn't know what it was, so I didn't know what to do. Still, I tried to apply solutions where I felt solutions were necessary. Many problems arose. It's hard to fix something when you don't know what you're fixing.

Acting like G.I. Joe when you're not G.I. Joe won't catch the bad guy, designing an airplane that won't ever fly won't get you to Disneyland, and being an air guitar rock star won't secure you a record deal. Life is nothing but frustrating when you're out of place. A lost child needs to be found. Seeing that there were no answers in the places I was looking, I turned an extreme corner. I was only seven years old when I started doing drugs.

I was told that smoking marijuana makes you cool. I desperately wanted to be cool; I was awkward, too smart, and too skinny. The kids in second grade picked on me. The idea of doing something that "cool people" were doing seemed like a good one. In 1973, cool people smoked pot. Smoking pot was going to transform me somehow—and I was transformed immediately. I now had a label: I was a pot smoker. I then found other pot smokers, other kids just like me who had also turned an extreme corner. Those of us who were lost were no longer lost; we were second-grade stoners. This seemed to make everything okay. Life became a kind of joke.

Someone once painted the words LEGALIZE POT on the side of our school. People were appalled, but we were thrilled. We shared in that secret. People could look at our lives from the outside, but they certainly weren't going to get on the inside. Look who's awkward now. The fantasy played out in my head: I was a real-life bad guy. The law hunted people like me.

My friends and I would sit in the woods and get stoned, or walk down the street and get stoned. We got stoned hanging out of our bedroom windows, and we got stoned hiding in people's backyards. We almost always had drugs in our pockets. We were wild and dangerous.

One time, some big kids showed up and chased us out of the woods. They told us to never come back. If they would have really considered what they were doing, they probably would've thought twice. We saw the kids again when they came to buy weed from the same kid we were buying from. But they didn't say anything to us; they didn't even know who we were.

CHAPTER 2
MISSED OPPORTUNITIES

I CAN LOOK back now and see the times when everything could've changed. There are particular moments in life where the momentum stops, and an opportunity to travel a different path arises. The window to access these moments is finite, though; it closes soon enough. Inevitably, other moments do arrive, but if you're not paying attention, they will close on you too.

For some people, a certain thing occurs. Years pass, and all of life's particular moments pass. The pattern of today is the pattern for tomorrow, and for the next day, and the next. I understand what this is like because it happened to me. I often found myself dwelling in an unchanging place.

I was running from the inevitable pains of growing up, but painful things kept occurring. I was baffled. As much as I diligently strove to be comfortable, I still felt uncomfortable. I thought surely I would find a place where I would feel good most of the time. It didn't dawn on me that places like that might not look familiar to me. You can mislead yourself when you're sure you have the answers. It's easy to travel in a perilous direction.

I was trying to bury what I felt, but it wasn't working. The darkness doesn't always kill what you think it would. A seed grows when covered by dirt. Perhaps if I could have just stopped, then the things that were chasing me would've turned and ran. But it's impossible to do sometimes.

So, I skipped on the chance to learn to shoot baskets, I was absent the evening when my crush sat alone, and I hid when the bully would've lost the fight. My methods could be quite thorough. Sometimes, though, I just allowed myself to be a kid.

My friends and I would take our allowances, and instead of going to the mall, we would board a train to New York City. Five twelve-year-old Jersey kids wandering in New York City in the late seventies could be pretty risky, but was definitely exciting. Back then, New York wasn't the place that it is today. A kid who didn't know what he was doing could get hurt. It's a good thing there was a gang of us. We were quite a crew; we never got hurt, and we had a good time.

We watched the people lose their money playing three-card monte. We ate spectacular hot dogs bought right on the street corner. We went to the Empire State Building, the Statue of Liberty, and the Twin Towers. We watched Ranger games at Madison Square Garden, gasped at the dinosaurs in the American Museum of Natural History, and roamed the great hills of Central Park. Life can be so unusual. It's probably exactly what you need, and you don't ever see it. It can be impossible to see sometimes.

CHAPTER 3
IF I ONLY KNEW THEN

WHEN MY TEEN years entered the picture, I spent most of the time getting high. I found myself mingling with one of the many "wrong crowds" in our neighborhood. The wrong crowd was the right crowd for me, though. I finally learned how to not get picked on. I became friends with the toughest kids in town. Other kids who got picked on couldn't do this, but since I did drugs, and since tough kids liked drugs, I was able to pull it off. I would show up at someone's house and whip out a bag of weed, or perhaps some quaaludes, or maybe some mescaline, and the people who normally would've hated me suddenly liked me. Needless to say, my drug use had been escalating.

I found that I often felt scared with this crowd, but none of that mattered once I got high. Eradicating my emotions gave me the ability to be anywhere with anyone. Throughout a typical evening, fistfights would ensue, sex would be available for most, responsibility was forbidden, and brain cells were disposable. My mind would eventually cease operations, taking with it the ability to realize that I just wanted to leave. People started to get used to me being in the state I was in. I was usually quiet, and often sad, but I acted happy. Everyone thought I was just crazy, and somewhat out of place, but as time went on, a good reason to stick around was becoming obvious to me: I really needed something to fix what I was, and fix it right away.

The difficulties that had always been present with me were maturing. I was attracted to girls, but too shy to do anything. I was naturally athletic, but just sat around. I was good in school, but screwed off anyway. Life seemed to be full of confusing and stressful hypocrisies. I was sinking deep down to a place that I did not want to be.

So, I turned to my friends for the solution. I was never very far from my friends. They were going to teach me, since they had it all figured out. They never seemed to go through the problems that I was going through.

I imagined how I would soon feel, what I would say, what I would do. I imagined how cool I was going to be. This was going to work.

I would go to a party and sit on the couch. Everything would smell like beer and smoke. Every light in the house would be on full blast. In the backyard, there would be laughter and occasional screams of approval for what someone had said. In the kitchen, people would smoke everything and sniff lines of everything. Friends would occasionally wander into the living room, having some conversation made difficult to hear by the music. They

might ask how I was. I was "good, doing great; I'm fine."
"Yeah, cool, see you later." What awesome fun.

I once watched the girl I loved most sitting across from
me, making out with some guy. They were really going at it.
It was time to go now. I had seen enough.

Usually afterwards, I would lie in bed, feeling my
heart as it pounded out of my chest. I had done what
everybody else did that night. I went where they went, I
talked when they talked, I laughed when they laughed, I
listened to the music they listened to, and now I was home
alone, reflecting. I was good at reflecting, and I was good at
being alone. I could plan out tomorrow when I was alone.
Tomorrow could be completely different; I just needed to
do things differently tomorrow.

CHAPTER 4

WONDER YEARS

TOMORROW EVENTUALLY CAME, and now that I was old enough to drive, my driver's license. This was a great opportunity for me. We could finally cop some really good acid. A place in the Bronx was turning up quality stuff, and we started dropping it pretty regularly. I had reached a point of no return by now. The drugs were doing their job. I certainly was becoming different. Dropping acid was an integral part of everything that my friends and I did.

We had it all figured out: just stay as high as you can, as often as you can, on the best stuff that you can get your hands on, and life is great. Whatever you need taken care of just seems to get taken care of. The girl you weren't with wasn't the important one, the fight you didn't have wasn't the right one, and being popular didn't matter. Your people might matter, but your drugs always mattered. I have to admit, I was starting to feel all right with the way things were. I could ignore just about anything that bothered me. I could play just about any role that I needed to play. Living like this could have been perceived as harmful, but to me, it was a pretty smart way to exist. I was finding my place within the ranks, and I became quite content to stay right where I was. But I had no idea where this was going to lead.

It became one party after another, drugs on top of more drugs, years and then more years. There is no new story to tell. I woke up every morning and just did what I did the day before. It could have been fine, except that I was no longer a teenager; I was now twenty years old. But there was hope: crack cocaine had just made its debut. It was 1986.

We found ourselves in New York City all the time now. We would usually end up in Times Square. Times Square was called Forty-Deuce back then, the nickname given to 42nd Street. We weren't hanging out in New York buying hot dogs like we used to, though; we were there to buy crack. There were no more museums, Ranger games, or Statue of Liberty trips. Instead, we hung out amongst the people selling switchblades, fake IDs, and their well-worn bodies. The once crazy young kids from Jersey had turned into the crazy crackhead kids from Jersey. This was not a good idea, and I knew it—but I did it anyway.

Then, I don't exactly know what happened, but something became clear to me: something needed to change. I wasn't feeling quite right. I believed I was partying way too much. There had to be another destiny in store for me. So, I came up with a plan. I partook in one of the greatest and quickest life fixes there is: I joined the military.

Joining the military has great potential to straighten a young person out. I learned to fix airplanes in the military, and I got to travel the world, but still, I was partying way too much. There were no drugs around, but there was plenty of alcohol, and my friends and I drank every night.

Those days quickly became some of the most fun days of my life. I drove a cool Trans-Am, a fast motorcycle, and even a classic convertible Chevy for a little while. Important stuff for a young man trying to impress a crowd.

There was lots of dancing, huge parties in hotel rooms, and many nights spent going to rock & roll shows. We were always with each other, and I always had a girlfriend. I was rarely alone. What people say about military friends is true: I grew very close to these people.

But just as quickly as it had begun, it was over. My enlistment was up. Four years went by really fast, and I was ready to leave. I was definitely partying way too much. I felt there was another destiny in store for me, so I went back home.

CHAPTER 5
HOME SWEET HOME

MY FRIENDS BACK home were not the same as when I left. I wasn't met with the crazy welcome I had expected, but instead with excuses. No one wanted to go out and drink with me. People had to work, or had a wife waiting at home, or had a kid on the way. I was usually left to close down the bar by myself. It might have been a problem, except that I learned to drive with one eye closed. Seeing double became less of a big deal then, and drunk driving was rendered manageable.

However, I still searched for people to do things with, so I started hanging out with an old friend from high school. He had gotten into smoking crack. I was okay with that. It was just like old times for me. We would smoke crack and sit under a workbench in his garage, not talking. I did this for a while, but it got to be too expensive. When I stopped smoking crack with him, I never saw him again.

One time I went to the beach with the girl I loved the most. This was finally my chance. We got drunk at a bar and walked along the sand. It was chilly, and we got close, then we kissed, and that was that. I was tired, my buzz wore off, and we drove home. It seemed like the right time to leave. I didn't see her anymore after that. Apparently I didn't love her as much as I used to.

Then there was my best friend from the earliest days. He and I went way back. We had known each other since we were kids, and we had solid history. I expected that we would have great times together. We hung out, we had a ton of fun, and then I met someone: the girl of my dreams. I started spending a lot of time with this girl—all my time. My friend expressed to me that it might be too much. I didn't understand why he didn't understand that I had a girlfriend. I found there wasn't much of a reason to stay friends with him after that.

Meeting someone you really like is one of the most beautiful experiences in life. There's not much that compares to that particular excitement and happiness. I love the rush when it happens. I love the hope that it may last. The hope can be precarious, though, and the rush is notoriously temporary. However, there is always the thought, *Not this time. There's a special someone out there for everyone.* I felt it; I was in the place where that occurs. My new girlfriend and I had a great time for quite a few years. I didn't know at that time just how fake I really was.

At the end of the day, the fear, pain, and uncertainty I had felt my whole life hadn't changed. I acquired many skills to suppress how I felt, but I acquired very few skills to express how I felt. This became clear whenever I needed to be vulnerable. Now was the time, but it was not going to happen. My guard was up like never before; I could not let her see me for the scared person I really was. She certainly would leave me. I never saw my part in anything.

Smoking cigarettes until my lungs hurt, drinking coffee until my stomach was in knots, masturbating all night long, and consuming alcohol until I threw up always seemed to fix things for me. It was time to accelerate them all. It was time to destroy whatever this was inside of me. But ultimately, the only thing I destroyed was the relationship.

When having sex with yourself becomes more important than having sex with your partner, there's remorse and isolation. When spending all your money getting drunk becomes the normal thing that you do, there's anxiety and regret. When your health is so compromised that you can't sleep or eat, you need to get help, or die. So, I sought counseling, and confessed to the counselor what I thought was best for him to know. I told him about my drinking. He suggested that I stop drinking while I was coming to see him, and I tried, but I just couldn't. He then had a solution for me. He believed I was an alcoholic, and that I should seek proper help. My counseling days were over. In accordance with his advice, I attended an outpatient rehab program and started going to AA meetings.

CHAPTER 6
HITTING BOTTOM

BEING DIAGNOSED AS an alcoholic was great news to me. I had begun to think that I was hopelessly defective. When you're an alcoholic, you can sit in a room with other alcoholics, listen to their stories of self-destruction, share your own stories of self-destruction, work a spiritual program known as the twelve steps, and stop drinking with this process. You find that you're not hopelessly defective, but have a disease known as alcoholism. The disease is treated by going to meetings, listening, getting involved, and being honest.

I went to meetings, I listened, and I got involved—but being honest was another thing altogether. My definition of honesty was telling a story that you believed. It didn't matter if the story was true or not. Life seemed to be easier this way. Everything came out exactly as I thought it should have.

I was told to go to a lot of meetings. I went to a meeting just about every day, but something wasn't working. I could only stay sober for a few months at a time. I surmised the problem was that I was too young; a lot of the people I met in meetings were older than me. I felt like maybe I was trying to put a cast on a bone that was not yet broken. I had to do something. So, I decided it was time to go break some bones.

I stopped going to AA and drank more than ever. Every night, I sat in the corner of a bar and watched people have a good time. Couples came and went, and groups of friends came and went. Older people were usually there early, and younger people showed up late. I was there for it all. I found that strip clubs were a great place for me to go; it wasn't unusual for someone to sit alone in a strip club. I drank a lot in strip clubs.

One afternoon, I met two young women at a strip club. They were so pretty and young, and they were interested in me. I was out of shape, unshaven, and dressed like a slob, so two young ladies liking me seemed pretty strange to me, but indeed, it was happening. I went home with them and found that they were two of the most laid-back people I had ever met. They didn't seem to care about anything. I wanted to know more. I wanted to be the way they were.

To be the way that they were turned out to be easy, as they were junkies. All I had to do was start doing heroin, and then I could be the same way. I tried it, and I instantly liked it. All my anxiety immediately went away. All of the fear, pain, and uncertainty vanished. It looked as if I had broken the right bone, and that maybe this bone should just stay broken. I had tried many methods to change what I was, but this method obliterated what I was. It convinced me that this was what I had always needed. I fully bought in. It didn't take long for me to become addicted.

It's quite an ordeal when you're addicted to heroin. If you don't have your drug, you get really sick. It feels like a very bad flu, coupled with a lot of pain, along with a very bad attitude, only terribly worse. It's crazy to even describe. One thing becomes clear, though: you have to have heroin just to be okay. As a result, you become part of a culture.

There was a rule that we of this culture followed: a junkie doesn't let his or her fellow junkies get sick, and that's about it. Not long after I met the two girls, one ended up in jail, and one moved away, and that was fine. I quickly found new people to use heroin with, and I was schooled in the life of a junkie.

It was impressed upon me that we took care of each other's habits, but it was okay to steal from your friends. It was okay to watch your friends get busted. It was okay, too, if someone got beat up. It was even okay if someone overdosed. This is just the way it was.

Eventually, everyone I was with either got locked up or moved away, and the lifestyle was becoming pretty difficult. Times became truly desperate. I was in my thirties now, I was a junkie, I was completely alone, and I became scared. I felt that the end was near.

The young lady I knew from the strip club that had moved away eventually moved back, and we started running the streets again, only now everything was worse. Our addictions were worse, our health was worse, our money problems were worse, and we were miserable unless we were high all the time. It's hard to stay high all the time. One day, she suggested that we should get clean, that maybe we needed help, that maybe we should go to a meeting, and I agreed. So, we went to Alcoholics Anonymous, as that was all I knew of help, but we were out of place there. We weren't alcoholics; we were heroin addicts. So, we went to a Narcotics Anonymous meeting, then went our separate ways, and then something happened. The next chapter was about to begin.

CHAPTER 7

THERE'S HOPE YET

NARCOTICS ANONYMOUS WAS different from Alcoholics Anonymous. The focus of the AA meetings I attended was mainly alcohol, but in NA meetings, you could drink too much, smoke crack too much, shoot heroin too much, snort cocaine too much, or do just about anything too much, and you were considered to be an addict who needed help. I liked the liberal attitude that dominated NA, and as a result of this attitude, the diverse crowds that I saw there. People gathered no matter what their level of depravity. I wanted more, so I kept showing up, and as a result, I was staying clean.

It didn't remain that easy, though.

I wasn't getting what I needed for the long haul. I found that my emotions were going awry at nearly every turn. I would be angry one moment, then happy the next. I was depressed one moment, then ecstatic the next. I hated everybody and everything one moment, and then I loved everybody and everything the next. I craved a break, and I tried what I knew.

But smoking two packs of cigarettes every day didn't help, drinking five cups of coffee every day didn't help, sleeping too much didn't help, sleeping too little didn't help, and sex didn't help.

Every substitute I tried did fill the hole left behind from not using drugs, but it did little for the unruly, unstable, racing mind that I was dealing with. I believed I would relapse if I didn't dig deeper. Terrified by this possibility, I went to a meeting every night.

On one particular night, I was listening to someone share about their kids, their partner, and I'm not sure what else, and I got so angry. Here I was attending a Narcotics Anonymous meeting, trying to stay clean, and here was this person sharing about the day they had with their family. My mind was just as volatile as ever. I had to do something about this.

I raised my hand and shared how mad I was. I shared about how I didn't even have kids or a partner, and how all I wanted to do was stay clean, and I didn't know how I was supposed to do that by listening to things that had nothing to do with drugs. Afterwards, people came up to me and thanked me for sharing. They said they often had thoughts like mine. They told me I would be all right, to keep coming back, and to just keep doing what I was doing. I was surprised; I thought I had offended the whole room. I thought I had certainly made people mad at me. I felt like I might even be exiled for what I had said. Instead, people allowed me to own what I said, realized that it came from the heart, accepted it for what it was, and accepted me for what I was. I actually felt relieved, even pretty good.

So, I started sharing all the time. I shared about my thoughts, my feelings, my fears, my anger, and my troubles. I talked about the things that were bothering me. I didn't realize it, but I was doing something that I hadn't done before: I was being real and honest. I was unveiling myself before a crowd.

Soon I started making friends in NA and began to do a lot of things with these friends. We went to the movies, took road trips, went bowling, played cards, had barbecues, and attended NA dances. At times, dozens of us would take over the local diner, spending hours just talking. Many of us were in relationships, and many of these relationships turned into marriages. People experienced miraculous changes in their lives. They bought their first houses, graduated from college, got good jobs, had children, and genuinely fell in love. People were finding their place in the world. I saw it all, and naturally, I assumed that my turn would come.

I was not to share in that bliss, though. I did achieve many of the things that others achieved, but success in the material world did little for me. It was difficulty in relationships that was perhaps the most painful.

Even though I was with many friends, I felt as if I barely knew anyone. Even though I was invited to do many things, I often didn't want to go. Even though I went on plenty of dates, I found that I wasn't that interested in romance, and this really hit home. I tried dating short-term, I tried dating long-term, and even fell in love at least once or twice, but I still preferred to be by myself. I could not understand why things were the way they were. I needed some answers. I was forty-one years old now. It was time to dig even deeper.

CHAPTER 8
A FUTURE

I STARTED READING a lot of books. I was searching for a way to make myself feel better. I was reading mainly psychology stuff. There was one book that was different, though. I'm not even really sure where it came from. It was a book of poetry by the ancient Sufi mystic, Rumi. There was something intriguing about this book. It didn't talk about the way I felt; it talked about the way that people saw things. Staying clean eventually leads many if not most people down a spiritual path. I believed that this is what was going on with me. So, I kept reading Rumi.

Rumi's poetry is exotic and fun to read. He speaks of ecstasy, love, miraculous beings, supernormal experiences and humankind along with it all. Rumi describes a world where mysterious and seemingly unrelated things come together as one. The possibility was intriguing. It was a hopeful one for me. I considered that there might be a state of existence unlike anything I had known before.

I eventually decided that I should move on from Rumi, though, and I started reading even more. I read Eckhart Tolle and really liked what he had to say. I also read books on the teachings of the Buddha, and I immediately noticed something: Eckhart Tolle and the Buddha seemed to present similar ideas. I felt as if this helped legitimize both of them, but it created a dilemma for me. I wanted to dedicate myself to one method of study, but I could not decide if it should be what the Buddha taught, or what Eckhart Tolle teaches. I ultimately chose the Buddha. There was a lot more Buddhist material to work with.

I went on to read books on Japanese Buddhism, Chinese Buddhism, Tibetan Buddhism, and even Buddhism in relation to twelve-step recovery. Something about it was grabbing my attention, but I was struggling. Some of what I read was just too weird for me, and a lot of what I read seemed too technical. I didn't give up, though.

I eventually found a piece of Buddhist literature called *The Noble Eightfold Path: Way to the End of Suffering*. It was written by a monk named Bhikkhu Bodhi. This was different from the other Buddhist literature I had been reading. It seemed accessible and practical. Most importantly, it seemed like it could be life-changing.

Energized and inspired, I found more to read. I bought a book called *In the Buddha's Words: An Anthology of Discourses from the Pali Canon*. I liked this book quite a bit. I checked the author and saw that it, too, was written by Bhikkhu Bodhi. I wanted to learn more about this man. It turned out that Bhikkhu Bodhi would often stay at a monastery in North Jersey that I could visit, as it wasn't very far from my home.

One afternoon, I called the monastery to find out if I could get a tour. The man who answered the phone told me that they didn't give tours. He mentioned that they did offer a free class every Tuesday, though, in which they went over teachings from the *Majjhima Nikaya*. I had no idea what that was. He told me the *Majjhima Nikaya* is part of one of the oldest and most authentic collections of the Buddha's teachings known to exist. He said that if I wanted to attend the class, he could get me a copy of that Tuesday's teaching.

I agreed and asked how I could find him. He said to just come in the front door, and he would be somewhere nearby, since he was the teacher of the class. My curiosity was starting to peak. When he told me his name, I practically fell out of my chair; it was Bhikkhu Bodhi. Bhikkhu Bodhi had answered the phone.

The class was fantastic. Bhikkhu Bodhi is brilliant. The *Majjhima Nikaya* was amazing to me. I immediately fell in love with its teachings, and went out and bought the book.

I started reading the *Majjhima Nikaya* every morning, and began attending Bhikkhu Bodhi's class every chance I could. The book ended up being deeper than I thought it would be, though. Having access to the class was a great blessing, and did help a lot, but I was still mystified by much of what I read. I read some paragraphs over and over just trying to understand them. Clearly, I was going to need to do more than just read.

The *Majjhima Nikaya* regularly mentioned meditation, and I didn't know what it would accomplish, but I knew what I was going to do. So, I finished the Red Bull I was drinking, put out the Newport Light I was smoking, sat on my living room floor, and meditated.

BOOK 2

MICHAEL IS BORN

THIS IS UNCOMFORTABLE

The time is now, and I don't really know what
I'm doing. Every morning I wake up, I read the
Majjhima Nikaya, and I sit in a recliner and
meditate. I like the recliner. There's a little round
table with a mosaic top next to it that I can sit my
coffee and cigarettes on. I sit straight up in the
recliner, close my eyes, and then I just sit here.

I heard that meditation was supposed to
be peaceful. I don't understand how it could
not be peaceful; you're not doing anything. I
do understand how it could be boring, though;
you're not doing anything. It is not boring for
me, but neither is it peaceful. The past is here,
the future somehow happens to be here, and the
present is everywhere but here.

I have chosen to persist. I've made the
decision to meditate every day for five years. I
thought that if after five years, the meditation
did nothing for me, then I would stop. Five
years seems like a long time, but five years is my
chosen number. The peace comes and goes, and

being bored is never the case, but something is changing. I'm starting to look at the world differently. I'm starting to think about things I had not thought about before.

CHAPTER 9

IGNORANCE

THE SIDEWALK BENEATH my feet is disintegrating, but I don't consider this. The sun is running out of fuel, but I look away from this. Every day I am dying, but healthy, so I don't think about this. I see what's going on.

I work to find solace when things are stressful, but things are still stressful. I strive to feel pleasure when things are painful, but things are still painful. I want to make my self known, but what I am remains unknown. Everything is disintegrating and decaying and will eventually die, and I am spending all my time trying to create an existence that's peaceful and stable. Any living creature will clearly tell the truth, though. An alteration of what you are can occur in an instant. My thoughts effectively provide me with something to ponder.

I often sit still, steadying my mind, trying to hold onto a thought. Right now, I'm picturing a bicycle, and trying to keep the thought of the bicycle in clear focus. I'm trying to see how long the image remains unaltered in my mind.

If I'm observant, I will see that the thought changes as soon as I think it. The bicycle thought or image is really a series of bicycle thoughts or images. Thoughts and images run together, creating the illusion of oneness. Even though this is what happens, I still miss the truth. I act as if I know what the right thing to do is.

It is that I allow the mind to create my world. Sights, sounds, smells, tastes, touches, and thoughts are always being noted, and finalized. I see forever as, "When I get back, things will be the way they are now." This is ignorance—and then there are the thoughts.

CHAPTER 10

FORMATIONS

THOUGHTS ARE NOTHING more than formations of the mind. My thoughts exist in their current form because I misunderstand the things that disappear. They come to me from within, and they exert influence. They could be interpreted as a reliable force, but they are fleeting.

I make decisions based on my thoughts. These decisions change my surroundings. Something that did not have to happen leaves its mark on the world.

I realize that these formations of the mind exist in three categories. There are bodily formations that pertain to the body; there are verbal formations that pertain to the thoughts themselves; and there are mental formations that pertain purely to the mind itself. I've found that when I look close enough, I can see their individual expressions.

When a sensation appears from a part of the body, I'm captured by its good or bad nature. *Here is a bodily formation.*

When a story is constructed from a group of thoughts, I'm devoted to the message it brings. *Here is a verbal formation.*

When an impulse arises from a certain instinct, I'm enchanted by its convincing sway. *Here is a mental formation.*

I don't perceive the world based upon the world, but based upon these three formations. I do not see this as an issue, so I commit. I do things. I exercise my will upon things. I try to mold life's circumstances into something that matches what comes from inside me.

I can interact with people without seeing how they feel, but only seeing how I feel. I can perform tasks in this life while not being inspired by the task, but only by the result that I would like. I can be a good person not because it's right to be a good person, but only because I choose to be a good person. This can be my motivation. It can be hard to see how out of touch it can be. It can be hard to admit that things can be like this.

CHAPTER 11
CONSCIOUSNESS

I AM CONSCIOUS of these formations of the mind. I am aware when a sensation appears from a part of the body, when a story is constructed from a group of thoughts, and when an impulse arises from a certain instinct. I explore how these formations affect me. A pleasant sensation, story, or impulse will leave an impression that's pleasant. A painful sensation, story, or impulse will leave an impression that's painful. A neither painful nor pleasant sensation, story, or impulse will leave an impression that's neither painful nor pleasant.

I understand there is good reason for me to be conscious of how things affect me. Most of us can only imagine how difficult life could be. Think what it was like for the earliest groups of people. Fierce predators had to be dutifully watched for, food and water had to be regularly gathered, and shelter had to be continually maintained. We're not necessarily equipped to deal with difficulties such as these. We possess no large fangs or claws, our skin is not very tough, we don't move especially fast, and we're not overly strong. For us to survive would require something extraordinary. But we indeed have something extraordinary. We notice what's around us, cultivate a perception of what just happened, remember the outcome, and do what we need to do to survive.

We draw conclusions and devise solutions. We identify weaknesses and cultivate advantages. We destroy obstacles and make improvements. We kill when we want to, preserve when we have to, and make friends when we can. This is how I see the world.

We think that our accomplishments must mean that what we do is right. It's easy to be right when being right means that you will live to see another day. We have taken it to another level, though; we've come to believe that the world is here to serve us, and this is not okay. We may find ourselves acting as if we are the most important.

I look at myself. If I perceive something as pleasant, I expect there to be more. If I perceive something as painful, I do not want it to happen again. If I perceive something as neither painful nor pleasant, I tend to just ignore what it really is.

Just picture how deep your feelings of desire can be when you like something, how strong your aversion can be when you don't like something, and just how unconcerned you can be when you're content. These states that arise can last far beyond the events that caused them, and this is where the problem occurs. I see that I am not present. My consciousness is being affected, but I believe that it's all under control.

CHAPTER 12

MIND AND BODY

LIFE WILL STILL do whatever it wants, though. However, we are creative beings. We come up with ideas, we see them as a unique part of ourselves, we feel the need to express our ideas, and we create the situations that we believe we're supposed to create. All people are creative in this way. Creativity is not limited to people such as painters or the sculptors. Personally, I am not a painter or a sculptor, but I do try.

I recently got a call from my sister. My sister and I don't always get along, but she is ill, so I went to see her. I just got back from what ended up being a nice visit. I was surprised that it went so well, considering that I had feared a regrettable encounter. I can complicate things even when there really is no reason to.

My sister, who is dying of cancer, had a different experience.

She was simply happy that I had come. She had mentioned to her daughter, my niece, how much it meant to her, and my niece called to tell me. I would not have guessed that my visit meant what it did. I wondered what was so horribly wrong with me.

It's important to say how it is. We are confronted by the world, we take in what we perceive, and then we act accordingly. I'm trying to do my best with what I have, and you're trying to do your best with what you have. It's often true that what seems to be the best may actually not be the best, and this is said to be okay, but things might not work out. There may not be many choices, though.

The traits that color our decision-making process have already been developed. As a result, I can react to what I go through in a favorable way, an unfavorable way, or perhaps somewhere in between. I don't like it when I react in a way that's unfavorable, but still, it happens. I may hurt someone in some fashion, or in the case of my sister, I hurt myself, while everyone else thinks that I'm noble. A lot of situations do turn out well. Most situations, however, just pass by. This is karma. We are all products of situations from the past, and we produce the situations of the future.

It's often without my acknowledgment that this karma occurs. I can be more unaware than not. I often don't know why I'm confused, depressed, angry, or sad, nor do I understand where happiness, joy, and the good times come from. I then operate in a specific way. I move amongst the details of my life not realizing that the outcome has already been determined. I believe that the unpredictable or the unacceptable is right around the corner, waiting to see how far I might go.

CHAPTER 13

THE FIVE SENSES AND THE MIND

IT IS DUE to the mind and the body that I go where I go. The mind has its game plan. It has its karma, and the body follows along. The mind gets what it gets from somewhere, though. We have five senses. There are the eyes, and the different sights that they see; the ears, and the different sounds that they hear; the nose, and the different odors that it smells; the tongue, and the different flavors that it tastes; and the body, and the different objects that it touches. Eyes, ears, nose, tongue, and body are internal, while sights, sounds, odors, flavors, and objects are external.

My involvement with everyone and everything happens in relation to what I see, hear, smell, taste, and touch. The five senses are the doorways that allow the world to visit the mind. The mind then determines how these guests are to be treated. As was the case with my sister, not all are welcomed easily. My mind will realize a certain guest has arrived, and throw up its defenses. These defenses can be unnecessary, but by then it's too late.

CHAPTER 14

CONTACT

I'VE ALREADY MADE contact with the world. With the best of intentions, I bravely engage with life. I know I play my part, but I don't always understand the people around me. I don't always connect. I view things differently from day to day.

On some days, people are the whole of my life, but on other days, I wish to be left alone. On some days, I am fully included, but on other days, I fail to leave my home. On some days, I speak very well, but on other days, my words just remain unknown.

Things are the way they are, and the effect of an act will remain the effect of an act, but still, the mind sees what it wants to see.

I can look at any person and determine that a request for connection is an act of selfishness, that a show of generosity is a display of manipulation, and that an expression of need is an admittance of weakness.

But I can also find raw honesty in what seems like meanness, true beauty in perceived ugliness, and healing solitude when there's loneliness. Something within me changes me. I feel something.

CHAPTER 15

FEELING

I FEEL PAIN, and I feel pleasure, and I feel neither pain nor pleasure. There is always a feeling, but it is unknown what that feeling will be from moment to moment. It could be said that probably every person desires mastery over their feelings. We may strive for success, romance, money, and beauty, but ultimately we just want to feel good, happy, or content. I pursue whatever I think will work.

In my life, I learned to turn to external things for the answers. We've all experienced success when we've acted this way. We know to look for food when we're hungry, shelter when we're cold, security when we're scared, and medicine when we're sick. We feel good when we're okay, and we feel bad when we're not okay. This mindset is a priority. The human animal was taught how to live. Most of us die having missed out on what this could mean.

Happiness can be pervasive, or happiness can be elusive, and when realized, it can leave too soon. The mind knows this, but does not necessarily understand this. I remember the things that I've been through, and I rely on my success a little too much.

I think I know how to find stability, but turning to external things is unreliable. Still, I continue. I look to the stars, turn my ears towards the song, taste the sweetness, smell the perfume, and touch what feels good. Our senses keep us busy, and they keep us fulfilled. They present to me these things that I'd like to pursue, but I know the relief won't last.

The way I live doesn't penetrate the fabric. It doesn't permeate the layers. It's difficult to sink down deep enough to see what truly needs to be seen.

When I sat with my girlfriend—how beautiful she is!—I experienced joy. When I sat with my boss and how disagreeable he is, I experienced anger. I sat with my life that day, and I wasn't sure if I really understood any of it. I live with my choices, and sometimes I wonder where these choices come from.

CHAPTER 16

CRAVING

I WANT TO be right, though. I insist that things can be the way that I want them to be. Even though the situations are obvious, I can pine for things to always work out. I crave to have things my way. If a person were ever fully satisfied, there would be no craving. I can't recall a time when I was ever fully satisfied. How I feel is always going away. To expect things to be different would be asking a lot. Some might say that it's an impossible aspiration.

Still, I don't accept the reality. My pursuit of pleasure can become relentless, and my retreat from pain is never-ending. The best way to live is easy.

So, I work to construct the times when I'll be okay, and to secure the times when I am okay, but nothing in the world stays committed to anybody.

Our minds convince us of just how special we are, though. Trees fall for our buildings, water spoils with our waste, animals die for our food, and we burn the planet with its own secretions.

You would think that we would understand how we live. We are unsure, though. We believe we are paramount, we believe we are the most important, but we are not. If we were the most important, then everything would listen to us.

Our minds and bodies would easily heal, our relationships would be effortless, and the world would thrive in the midst of our presence. Yet how different it is.

My mind and my body get sick at will, my relationships need work to be well, and the world is consumed until I've had my fill.

I crave for things to be the way I would like. This is a state of mind, and there is an appeal to it. I'm able to dream about what may be.

This human mind is amazing, powerful, curious, driven, always diligent, and so fully committed to our existence that we're able to concoct proof in something that would otherwise be known as untrue.

CHAPTER 17
CLINGING

SO, I END up misunderstanding this way that I am living. I don't accept that I'm really just getting into things and getting out of things, and I become too involved with what is happening.

I look for existence to be a particular way. When existence is as I want it to be, I enjoy it. When existence is not as I want it to be, I despair. I latch onto the good times, and dread the times when the bad will appear. Then I rebel against the bad times, and anticipate the times when the good will appear.

The other night, I was walking through the park. It was cold and rainy, and I was hurrying to get to my car. My hands were jammed in my pockets, and my hood was up. I looked straight down and walked very fast. *Ahh, it's so cold! I can't believe it's this cold... Ahh, it's so cold. The car is so far away...* The night before, I had been walking through the same park, and it was beautiful out. I saw people walking their dogs. I heard a person playing a guitar. I embraced the breeze on my skin. *It is so beautiful. I love when it's this beautiful! I love what I wrote tonight...* The next thing I knew, I was at my car.

I latch onto whatever I am feeling, and my view is that this is the right thing to do. I'm set in the ways that I deal with that particular situation, and I create a state of mind that is who I think I am.

But I'm playing a game. I seek out some stimuli, run from other stimuli, and then rage over my choices. I go in many different directions, and the next thing you know, the day is over.

I've created schemes that sometimes work out. However, there is usually something left undone, and this is what I soon will become.

CHAPTER 18

BECOMING

I BECOME SOMETHING. Look at how craving, clinging, and becoming work together. Craving is an idea of how one would like to exist, clinging is an attempt to keep a craving real, and becoming is what happens once there is clinging.

Imagine a day when you're totally in sync with the world. You're young when the world's young, and you're old when the world's old. You're hot when the world's hot, and you're cold when the world's cold. You're free when the world's free, and you're sold when the world's sold. You're the same as everything else.

Your day is the world's day, and your night is the world's night. Your death is the world's death, and your life is the world's life. This is harmony.

If this were ever the case, I wouldn't need to crave for anything, because there isn't anything I would want. I wouldn't cling to anything, because there isn't anything for me to cling to. I wouldn't become anything, because there isn't anything to become that I haven't become already. It would be easy to live this way.

I'd be still as everything is still, and here as everything is here. I'd change as everything changes, and appear as everything appears. I'd be like the wind and the wave; I'd fly, and I'd float.

It's hard to be this way, though. We were all born, we're consumed with the good and the bad days of our lives, and then we age, we grow sick, and we die.

CHAPTER 19

BIRTH

IT STARTS WITH birth. Being born is often seen as the singular event that is the beginning of a person's life. This is true, but there's more to be found. One should be wary of limiting oneself.

People can be seen as nothing more than a shifting collection of details. Our blood always flows, our hearts always beat, and we're always breathing. There are positions that we sit in, stand in, or lie down in. We see, hear, touch, taste, and smell the world. We feel, we act, and we end up in different places. Every day there is something new. Every day, something is born.

Don't underestimate what goes on. A glance across the room could change everything. If you know what you're looking at, you just might understand. If you don't know what you're looking at, you might not understand. A decision will be made, and things might not turn out in your favor. So, base everything upon what you know, and then you'll be sure of what you do. The results will occur, and there will be a new moment. It happens over and over. It is an accumulation of such moments that brought us to this place.

The time always seems to come, though, where I grow confused. Ignorance runs this day. Still, I will think, as I must think to carry on. Thinking, however, affects the consciousness; remnants are left behind. My intentions will find their basis here, and found is my motivation to act. The senses play a role here, and the chance will come to finally do something. So, I act, and now it's done. I feel, and there are effects. I wanted this, but it's not enough. But it must be good, so I won't let go. I am now stuck, and reality is false. We are all born, but I am lost.

My life is on its course. I didn't know that I chose my mentors, my health, my faculties, and my environment. I am only responding to what I feel is important, sometimes getting it right, and sometimes getting it wrong. This is the process. We're all moving toward the inevitable.

We'll build some houses beautiful, and we'll build some houses ugly; we'll build some houses big, and we'll build some houses small; we'll build some houses with love, and we'll build some houses with hate. We spend our whole life building houses. Look around. But in the end, they will all eventually fall down.

CHAPTER 20

AGING AND DEATH

BEING BORN INEVITABLY leads to aging and death. We know this. However, people still fear aging and death, but this should be expected. Aging and death are the ultimate unknown, and people react.

Effort goes into trying to control those things that may turn out in any number of ways. Aging and death, though, are always going to fulfill their roles. This doesn't mean that we're helpless, but we may not be wise.

I'm concerned with the loss of vigor and health, but aging makes my bones brittle, my back sore, and my eyesight poor. I'm concerned with the loss of the things that I care about, but death is a place where my friends cannot go, my possessions cannot go, and my body cannot go. You'll find that your concerns dictate how you live. Understand how this could turn out.

I recently watched my mother die. She was eighty-two years old. She had fallen and hurt herself and was unable to recover. While she was in the hospital, I was there every day. This allowed us to connect in the most meaningful of ways.

I talked with her while she was awake, and I sat with her while she was asleep. We did the things that kept her interested, and avoided the things that made her agitated. I knew when she needed something, and I knew when she didn't need something. I knew when she was lonely, and I knew when she just needed to be alone. I attended to her, and I made sure that she was cared for. I knew my mom my entire life. There wasn't much question as to what I was supposed to do.

I remember the day when she passed. She hadn't moved or opened her eyes for almost a week. I was very close by at this point. Then one afternoon, as I was sitting on a bench in front of the hospital, my mom's nurse called my cell phone. She told me I had better come inside right away. I rushed upstairs, and the nurse told me that it was time.

I entered my mom's room, and she was gasping for breath. Her eyes were tightly shut. Her whole body seemed incredibly tense. I couldn't believe what was going on. I was with my mom as she was about to die. I felt terrified and numb at the same time. Then my mom stopped breathing, opened her eyes, looked right at me, smiled the biggest, brightest smile—and she died.

"The Simile of the Raft" from the *Majjhima Nikaya* goes something like this:

Suppose a person in the course of a journey

saw a great expanse of water, whose near shore was dangerous and fearful and whose further shore was safe and free from fear, but there was no ferryboat or bridge for going to the far shore. Then the person thought: "There is this great expanse of water, whose near shore is dangerous and fearful and whose further shore is safe and free from fear, but there is no ferryboat or bridge going to the far shore. Suppose I collect grass, twigs, branches, and leaves and bind them together into a raft, and supported by the raft and making an effort with my hands and feet, I got safely across to the far shore." And then the person collected grass, twigs, branches, and leaves and bound them together into a raft, and supported by the raft and making an effort with their hands and feet, got safely across to the far shore. Then when they had got across and had arrived at the far shore, they might think thus: "This raft has been very helpful to me, since supported by it and making an effort with my hands and feet, I got safely across to the far shore. Suppose I were to hoist it on my head or load it on my shoulder, and then go wherever I want." Now what do you think? By doing so, would that person be doing what should be done with that raft? No. By doing what would that person be doing what should be done with that raft? Here, when that person got across and had arrived at the far shore, they might think thus: "This raft has been very helpful to me, since supported by it and making an effort with my hands and feet, I got safely across to the far shore. Suppose I were to haul it onto the dry land or set it adrift in the water, and then go wherever I want."Now, it is by so doing that that person would be doing what should be done with that raft.

My mom passed away in a way that was truly incredible. She appeared happy the moment she passed. She seemed to be genuinely okay with moving on. I know; I watched her die.

Still, I cried. I was going to miss my mom. I reflected on all that she and I had been through, but there were also things that I did not understand. There were questions left unanswered.

I wondered what had gone on right at the end. There was that smile; she exhibited such a beautiful smile just as she died. It was all that I could think about. I questioned if I could ever do what she did. I let much less important things worry me more than my mom's death seemed to worry her.

I didn't know it then, but my mom answered the questions that I was coming up with. She gave me an amazing parting gift. Her most elegant way of dying showed me exactly how to live.

THE CAUSE

After all of this, I'm still here. The state of being uncomfortable persists for me. When times are good, I have the idea that it is going to end. When times are bad, I have the idea that it is going to end. However, I am learning that there is a cause for everything.

It does make sense, but it's just an understanding, and not an answer. So, I am going to start to break things down.

CHAPTER 21
MATERIAL FORM

I AM MADE up of material from. Everything in this world is made up of material form. There are four elements that I like to explore: earth, air, fire, and water.

The earth element may be internal or external. The internal earth element is the hair, nails, skin, teeth, bones, kidneys, heart, liver, lungs, stomach, intestines, or whatever internally is solid and clung to. The external earth element is the earth itself, and both the internal and external earth element could simply be considered to be earth.

The air element may be internal or external. The internal air element is the air in the lungs, air in the belly, air in the bowels, or whatever internally is airy and clung to. The external air element is air itself, and both the internal and external air element could simply be considered to be air.

The fire element may be internal or external. The internal fire element is the warmth in the body, and that which utilizes the warmth in the body, such as digesting food or the healing of a wound, or whatever internally is warm and clung to. The external fire element is fire itself, and both the internal and external fire element could simply be considered to be fire.

The water element may be internal or external. The internal water element is blood, sweat, tears, saliva, urine, phlegm, or whatever internally is watery and clung to. The external water element is simply water itself, and both the internal and external water element could simply be considered to be water.

I was cutting my nails this morning, and one of them fell on the floor. Looking at it, I considered that just a moment ago, that was attached to me; that grew from me; that was a part of me.

I have a body. I believe that I own my body, but this is not true. My body is a part of everything else in the world. I have experiences. I believe that I own my experiences, but this is not true. My experiences are a part of everything else in the world. Everything that exists in this world is a part of this world.

I believe that I have it figured out, that I stand affirmed, and that I am as I am, but this is not true. Everything in this world comes and goes, and I come and go too. I am questioning my relationship to even that which may seem the most familiar to me.

CHAPTER 22

UNDERLYING TENDENCIES

I SEE THAT there are the different pleasant, painful, or neither painful nor pleasant experiences that I go through. This body that I inhabit can be affected, and it can be affected inappropriately. My mind can also be affected inappropriately. There can be three underlying tendencies present. There is greed, hatred, and delusion.

When I wish for pleasant experiences to remain longer than they do, greed is present. When I wish for painful experiences to leave sooner than they do, hate is present. When I don't see the neither painful nor pleasant experiences that happen in-between for what they really are, delusion is present.

What follows is "The Mistress and the Maid" from the *Majjhima Nikaya*:

> There was a housewife named Vedehika. And a good report about Mistress Vedehika had

spread thus: "Mistress Vedehika is kind, Mistress Vedehika is gentle, Mistress Vedehika is peaceful." Now Mistress Vedehika had a maid named Kali, who was clever, nimble, and neat in her work. The maid Kali thought: "A good report about my lady has spread thus: 'Mistress Vedehika is kind, Mistress Vedehika is gentle, Mistress Vedehika is peaceful.' How is it now, while she does not show anger, is it nevertheless actually present in her or is it absent? Or else is it just because my work is neat that my lady shows no anger though it is actually present in her? Suppose I test my lady."

So the maid Kali got up late. The Mistress Vedehika said: "Hey, Kali!" – "What is it, madam?" – "What is the matter that you get up so late?" – "Nothing is the matter, madam." – "Nothing is the matter, you wicked girl, yet you get up so late!" and she was angry and displeased, and she scowled. Then the maid Kali thought: "The fact is that while my lady does not show anger, it is actually present in her, not absent; and it is just because my work is neat that my lady shows no anger though it is actually present in her, not absent. Suppose I test my lady a little more."

So the maid Kali got up later in the day. Then Mistress Vedehika said: "Hey, Kali!" – "What is it, madam?" – "What is the matter that you get up later in the day?" – "Nothing is the matter, madam." – "Nothing is the matter, you wicked girl, yet you get up later in the day!" and she was angry and displeased, and she spoke words of displeasure. Then the maid Kali thought: "The fact is that while my lady does not show anger, it is actually present in her, not absent. Suppose I test my lady a little more."

So the maid Kali got up still later in the day. Then Mistress Vedehika said: "Hey, Kali!" – "What is it, madam?" – "What is the matter that you get up still later in the day?" – "Nothing is the matter, madam." – "Nothing is the matter, you wicked girl, yet you get up still later in the day!" and she was angry and displeased, and she took a rolling-pin, gave her a blow on the head, and cut her head. Then the maid Kali, with blood running from her cut head, denounced her mistress to the neighbors: "See, ladies, the kind lady's work! See, ladies, the gentle lady's work! See, ladies, the peaceful lady's work! How can she become angry and displeased with her only maid for getting up late? How can she take a rolling-pin, give her a blow on the head, and cut her head?" Then later on a bad report about Mistress Vedehika spread thus: "Mistress Vedehika is rough, Mistress Vedehika is violent, Mistress Vedehika is merciless."

The underlying tendencies of greed, hatred, and delusion lie in wait. When things are going well, it can be easy to behave well. When things are going poorly, it can be easy to behave poorly. When things are misunderstood, it can be easy to be confused. I am often confused when I'm having a good day, and then I'm not having a good day. It could be nothing more than a phone call, some news at work, news from home, or a trip to the doctor that changes everything. I have the ability to shift moods very quickly. The potential to act from a diminished state, bringing about diminished results, is ever possible. It may seem like there is little choice in how to act. This is not necessarily true.

I've come to understand that when I'm angry or hateful, it is due to an underlying tendency toward hate within me, and it doesn't have to be this way. I understand that when I'm desirous or greedy, it is due to an underlying tendency toward greed within me, and it doesn't have to be this way. I understand that when I'm deluded or confused, it is due to an underlying tendency toward delusion within me, and it doesn't have to be this way. I understand that it all happens in the moment, and there is more to how this all works.

CHAPTER 23

THE FIVE AGGREGATES AFFECTED BY CLINGING

IT CAN BE difficult to know that I am in the moment. It can be difficult to understand what exactly is going on. Something hidden may be uncovered. Instinctually I know that avoidance is wrong, but there is denial that I'm not living genuinely. I remember the story of Mistress Vedehika. The truth of how a person really is will sooner or later be expressed.

The reality might have to embark on a journey before it's recognized, though. There are processes that operate behind the scenes. There are the five aggregates affected by clinging.

There is the material form aggregate affected by clinging, the feeling aggregate affected by clinging, the perception aggregate affected by clinging, the formations aggregate affected by clinging, and the consciousness aggregate affected by clinging.

Material form is everything derived from the four elements of earth, air, fire, and water. I know that I am made up of material form, and that I'm going to make contact with material form.

Feeling is the pleasant, painful, or neither pleasant nor painful feeling that arises within me as a result of this contact.

Perception is an evaluation that I then make. I will perceive a contact to be good, bad, or neither good nor bad, based upon how I feel.

Then there are formations. I define formations here as the thoughts I am having as a result of perception. I'll think about the places that I find myself in.

Finally, there is consciousness. I am conscious of what is going on, and this stays with me.

The five aggregates affected by clinging provide an explanation of why we are the way we are. They will occur as long as we are alive in a body.

One day, I was sitting in a café, writing. The mood was chaotic. People talking loudly were a constant distraction. No matter how hard I tried, I could not concentrate. I was unable to accomplish what I was there to do, so I left the café.

On another day, I was sitting in a café, writing. The mood was subdued. There was a light rain falling outside. Concentration came easily, and I was focused. I was able to accomplish what I was there to do, so I stayed at the café.

There is material form. I make contact with material form when I'm sitting in a cafe.

There is feeling. Contact with loud people can bring up a feeling of anger or frustration, whereas contact with light rain can bring up a feeling of joy and calm.

There is perception. My respective negative or positive views of a situation will determine what happens next.

There are formations. I thought about leaving the café on the chaotic day, and I left. I thought about staying at the café on the rainy day, and I stayed.

There is consciousness. Events, once experienced, will never change from what they originally were.

It will then happen again in one fashion or another. Leaving a café will bring about contact, a feeling, a perception, and formations, and I will be conscious of what just happened. Staying in a café will bring about contact, a feeling, a perception, and formations, and I will be conscious of what just happened.

We bring the past with us. A moment of disappointment invites disappointment to enter into a new moment. A moment of fulfillment invites fulfillment to enter into a new moment. I can think what I want to think. I can think that I'm able to determine what the current moment is going to be. I might wish or even plead for things to be the way I want, but the current moment has already been determined.

Over time, I can start to believe that I'm just a certain kind of person. Suppose, however, that it is the five aggregates affected by clinging that are painting the picture of what we are. They have been with us since the beginning, but they change with the circumstances. They are impermanent.

CHAPTER 24

THE SELF

SINCE THE BEGINNING, I have had eyes through which I see this world. I see now that the eyes and the visuals that they see are impermanent. Therefore, the feelings, perceptions, thoughts, and consciousness that arise as a result of the eyes and what they see are impermanent.

I have had ears through which I hear this world. I see now that the ears and the sounds that they hear are impermanent. Therefore, the feelings, perceptions, thoughts, and consciousness that arise as a result of the ears and what they hear are impermanent.

I have had a nose through which I smell this world. I see now that the nose and the odors that it smells are impermanent. Therefore, the feelings, perceptions, thoughts, and consciousness that arise as a result of the nose and what it smells are impermanent.

I have had a tongue through which I taste this world.

I see now that the tongue and the flavors that it tastes are impermanent. Therefore, the feelings, perceptions, thoughts, and consciousness that arise as a result of the tongue and what it tastes are impermanent.

I have had a body through which I touch this world. I see now that the body and the objects that it touches are impermanent. Therefore, the feelings, perceptions, thoughts, and consciousness that arise as a result of the body and the objects that it touches are impermanent.

I have a mind through which everything comes together. I see now that the mind and the processes that it uses are impermanent, but I don't accept that they are impermanent.

This world is unsafe, unreliable, and not predictable. I have an unwillingness to exist where things are unsafe, unreliable, and not predictable, so I scrutinize form, interpret feelings, decide what I like, come up with a plan, and am ultimately going to be left with what happens.

I am going to be prepared. I am going to become the person I need to be to get where I need to go. I am not going to be caught off guard. I can be a nice guy, an angry guy, a sentimental guy, a judgmental guy, or whatever guy I need to be, depending on the situation. I can't help it. There is an aftereffect, though—Michael is born.

CHAPTER 25

MARA AND
THE BUDDHA

THE BUDDHA WAS born Siddhartha Gautama. Siddhartha had been engaged in spiritual practice for seven years when he found himself meditating under the bodhi tree. This was the night that he would reach enlightenment, the night that he would become the Buddha. He had just been on a life-changing journey.

Siddhartha had started out his life as a prince, and for his first twenty-eight years, he lived an especially privileged existence. He had riches, palaces, servants, lovers, and entertainers at his disposal. He enjoyed a multitude of princely comforts. Siddhartha's father, King Suddhodana, wanted it this way. He wanted his son to never desire anything other than to be a king like him someday. As a result, Siddhartha almost never left the palace that he lived in.

However, he grew tired of being in the palace all the time, and he decided to take a trip one day. He summoned his attendant, Channa, and together they ventured to a nearby town.

They came upon a person suffering from old age. Siddhartha was shocked. Having grown up the way that he did, he had never seen a person suffering from old age. He asked Channa, "What is wrong with that person?" Channa explained that it was a person suffering from old age, and that many people grow old and suffer.

They then came upon a person suffering from sickness. Siddhartha was again shocked. Having grown up the way that he did, he had never seen a person suffering from sickness. He asked Channa, "Now what is that? Is that old age?" Channa then explained that it was a person suffering from sickness, and that many people get sick and suffer.

They then came upon a dead body, bloated and rotting. Siddhartha was again shocked. Having grown up the way that he did, he had never seen a dead body, bloated and rotting. Siddhartha asked, "Channa, now what is that? Is that old age? Is that sickness?" Channa then explained that it was a dead body, bloated and rotting, and that every person's body will eventually become that way.

Finally, they came upon a person quietly meditating. Siddhartha asked, "Channa, what is that person doing?" Channa explained that it was a person meditating, and that the person was a recluse. He told Siddhartha that some people give up all that they have, renounce their mundane lives, and meditate, hoping to find peace and answers to what this life is all about.

Siddhartha was perplexed. He couldn't believe that he had never known of any of these things. He felt a bit let down, but instead of letting it affect him negatively, he used it for inspiration. He grew motivated and determined. Siddhartha decided that he was going to do something about all of this. So, he gave up his royal inheritance and left the palace to become a recluse. He was going to find out why this world is the way that it is. No one was able to stop him.

Siddhartha first sought out meditation teachers. He found two great masters. He studied under them and perfected their techniques. In Siddhartha's eyes, their practices fell short, though. So, he went looking for more.

He then teamed up with five recluses known for practicing severe austerities. Seeing the physical body as a hindrance to true knowledge, they tormented themselves. They wanted to overcome any attachment to the body. They lived out in the open, wore little clothing, barely ate, barely washed, and meditated all the time. Siddhartha adopted their practices, but found that their practices also fell short. Eventually, he just wandered off to practice alone.

He decided to become even stricter and more austere. He meditated constantly, had little contact with people, and nearly starved himself to death. He lost his hair, his skin shriveled, and he grew weak and sickly.

The Buddha said of these times, "I thought: 'Whatever recluses or brahmins in the past have experienced painful, racking, piercing feelings due to exertion, this is the utmost, there is none beyond this. And whatever recluses and brahmins in the future will experience painful, racking, piercing feelings due to exertion, this is the utmost, there is none beyond this. And whatever recluses and brahmins at present experience painful, racking, piercing feelings due to exertion, this is the utmost, there is none beyond this. But by this racking practice of austerities I have not attained any superhuman states, any distinction in knowledge and vision worthy of the noble ones. Could there be another path to enlightenment?'"

So, Siddhartha decided to give up the austerities and worked to regain his health. Having lived as a prince, he already knew that indulgence wouldn't provide the answers that he sought, and he now knew that denial would not either.

He recalled a time when he was a child.

Siddhartha was sitting under a rose apple tree, watching his father, and he experienced a great moment of clarity. This clarity took no effort. It didn't seem to be the result of anything that he was doing. It just came upon him from within. It was a powerful memory that had never left him. He wondered if this was in fact what he sought.

So, Siddhartha decided to find a peaceful place, and he sat under a tree, calmed his mind, and started to meditate. He was about to discover the Middle Way. It is the Buddhist Noble Eightfold Path that has been practiced ever since. He had company, though; Mara watched as Siddhartha meditated. He was there to stop Siddhartha from going any further.

Mara is a demon from Buddhist mythology. His purpose is to keep people stuck in the cycle of birth, aging, and death. Mara doesn't want anyone to arrive at the truth. He has a great number of tools at his disposal. Temptation, agitation, doubt, and fear are all used by Mara. Jealousy, anger, intolerance, greed, and anxiety are all the effects of his work. Mara has the ability to keep people very preoccupied.

It is said that Mara first tried enticing Siddhartha. He introduced Siddhartha to his three daughters. The true meaning of Mara's daughters remains open for debate. Commonly, though, they are thought to represent temptation, and most likely, sexual desire. They were supposed to convince Siddhartha to stop practicing. They were there to show him that there are seemingly better things that he could be doing. But the daughters failed. Siddhartha saw them for what they were, wished them away, and just quietly sat. Mara was surprised; this didn't often happen. He was far from done, though. He had much experience in keeping people trapped.

So, he tried intimidating Siddhartha. Mara attacked with an army of demons. Frightful images, thoughts, and ideas plagued Siddhartha. Pain and fatigue worked on him. Concentration was difficult, peace was strained, and any comfort was far removed. Siddhartha was under siege.

Siddhartha continued doing what he was doing, though. He had been through much during his years of practice. He had learned his strengths and weaknesses. He recognized the trouble that Mara was causing for him, and he continued meditating.

Mara was growing frustrated and angry. Siddhartha might actually find freedom. Mara wanted to end this right away. So, he chose to personally confront Siddhartha.

Mara screamed, "Stop! Stop doing what you are doing! This is going to cause you trouble! You don't want trouble, so I tell you to stop!" Siddhartha was unaffected. Mara screamed even louder, "Stop already, before you go too far! You will always be just how you are! You will never be free; forever deep is your scar!" Siddhartha, still unaffected, just looked at Mara. He understood that face, and he knew what Mara was there to do. Siddhartha looked down, touched the earth, and said, "I have practiced long and hard for just this moment." He looked up. "Mara, I know who you are, and know why you are here. I know who I am, and I know how I got here. My practice is dear; my mind is pure. My intentions are clear; my direction is sure. Take this body, and take this mind. You can have them; they are no longer mine. I am not affected by you, no matter what you do. I have no fear of you, as I now know what is true. I am free from you, now that I just saw all of you."

Then the earth and Siddhartha became one, and Mara knew he could do no more. He knew he had been defeated.

Thus the confrontation with Siddhartha stopped. Siddhartha's struggle ended, and he became enlightened. The Buddha had arrived.

There are different tellings of the Buddha's encounter with Mara. The accuracy of the story is not what's important here, but the lesson. Acceptance of demons isn't necessary. Acceptance of the Buddha's life isn't necessary.

76

Just look inward. All people have their Mara. This is what is necessary.

It is being seduced by things that don't have to seduce you, being wounded by things that don't have to wound you, and believing in things that really are not true that all create our Mara. People don't see what happens to them. When you let a demon be a demon, the demon becomes your demon—but this can change.

The Buddha touched the earth; we too can touch the earth.

THE END OF HOW IT WAS

My meditation is in a new place now. I am gaining a better understanding. An understanding and its application are two different things, though.

I am mostly peaceful now when sitting alone in my room, but I am not peaceful when I'm around most people. My spiritual practice seems incomplete. To feel peaceful around most people is a goal of mine. Fortunately for me, I live right outside New York City. There are a lot of people in New York City who meditate. I heard there is a meditation group in New York City that I might like.

CHAPTER 26

COMMUNITY

HERE I AM again. It used to be a group of alcoholics and junkies who were my friends. Then it was a group of recovering alcoholics and junkies who were my friends. Now it is a group of meditators who are my friends. One would think that a group of alcoholics and junkies would be a challenging group of friends. One might think that a group of recovering alcoholics and junkies would be a challenging group of friends. Not for me; I find a group of meditators to be a challenging group of friends.

Perhaps it is that my new friends are normal compared to what I'm used to. I don't know. I'm not sure I would know what normal looks like. I am starting to realize something, though.

I have friends who are okay with the madness, and friends who chase the sadness. I have friends who see the happiness, and friends who share in the randomness. I have friends who are here all the time, and friends who are here some of the time. I don't know that I always want to be around, but I do know that I'm going to stick around. There is a reason.

As much as I have loved my spiritual practice, it still can be unpredictable at times. The direction that I find myself pursuing often leads to an internal world. Many things come from the internal world. Painful memories arise; joyful possibilities arise. Hidden fears appear; revelations appear. Unannounced sadness is aroused; overwhelming rapture is aroused. I can share all of these experiences with my mediation group.

Still, there are the personalities. I often have trouble with personalities. I don't know why people do the things that they do. Still, there is my perseverance. I usually don't have trouble with my perseverance. I know why I must continue as I do. I feel like I have no choice.

One day, I started discussing the personalities with an experienced member of my group. She seemed to get along with everybody, and I thought she could help me. So, she became what one could call my teacher. A lot was shared between us, a lot was revealed, and a lot was understood. I can be good at one-on-one conversation. Being part of a community has proven to have its benefits.

Spiritual practice was a regular topic of discussion of ours. It became obvious that the time I spent practicing was quite extreme. I am willing to strive toward freedom more than many people do.

CHAPTER 27

THE FIVE FACTORS
OF STRIVING

IT IS JUST how it is. I do not think that my striving is some commendable act of exertion. Not to diminish exertion, as exertion is necessary, but I feel that spiritual practice is what I am well suited for. It's like an athlete in good shape playing sports all their life, a man with good looks finding a beautiful wife, or the intellect whose mind derives an answer that is right. When certain things are present, certain things can happen for people.

I've found that I truly believe in this practice that I do. I believe that the Buddha achieved freedom, and that it took work for him to reach that goal. I believe that if anyone puts in the necessary work, it is possible for them to also reach freedom. Understand that there were times when I felt that certain aspects of my character would never change. If I weren't able to place trust in the potency and viability of the Buddha and his teachings, I would not have continued to practice the way I have.

Honesty is necessary. One should admit when acting inappropriately toward oneself or others that it has lasting negative effects. One should also admit when acting appropriately toward oneself or others that it has lasting positive effects. Honesty for me is based on the reality of how I am treating myself and others, and I try to treat myself and others well.

A certain measure of health is needed to engage in practice. To be able to sit still in meditation for periods of time may seem physically simple to do, but a bad back, sore knees, an upset stomach, or a tired mind will hinder a person. I know that whenever I am sick, injured, overly tired, haven't eaten, or am just treating my body poorly, my ability to focus, be present, and remain undistracted when it is necessary is difficult. As a result, I am focusing on taking care of my health. I am treating myself better. However, when I am ill or afflicted and can do nothing about it, I acknowledge this mind and this body in their true and most fragile forms. Acceptance can be learned when this mind and body are acknowledged in their true and most fragile forms.

Practice also takes a specific kind of energy and understanding. There is the understanding of wholesome and unwholesome states, and there is the energy to cultivate what is appropriate. An understanding of wholesome and unwholesome states will change over time. It's not that wholesome or unwholesome states themselves change; their definition remains self-explanatory. Wholesome states create wholesome thoughts, words, and actions and do not cause harm. Unwholesome states create unwholesome thoughts, words, and actions and do cause harm. I apply energy toward cultivating wholesome states.

I look at how all of this applies. There is the increasing belief that there is something more than just what is presented to us by this world, or in other words, freedom, and there is the energy exerted to nourish an open state of mind. There is honesty in how one is acting toward oneself and others, and there is the energy applied to treat everyone well. There is the acceptance of one's mind and body in their true and most fragile forms, and there is the energy to try and build a healthy body and mind for one's practice. One has to start somewhere.

Then there is wisdom. Wisdom increases with practice. Initially, I only saw strength and weakness, capability and limitation, good points and bad points, but I am now starting to see things happening as they are happening. There is something inside of me that is behind what I am doing. I've found a purpose for self-compassion. Self-compassion can be the birth of wisdom, and wisdom can be the birth of compassion for others.

These are the five factors of striving: faith in the Buddha's teachings, honesty, taking care of one's health, the exertion of energy, and wisdom. I see these five factors of striving as ingredients. When I have a certain ingredient at a certain time, certain things will happen. When I don't have a certain ingredient at a certain time, certain things won't happen. There should be no judgment, since this is merely a fact. There are internal properties to practice that I pay attention to.

CHAPTER 28

THE FIVE PRECEPTS

THERE ARE EXTERNAL properties to practice that I pay attention to. I am coming to believe that effective spiritual development has a lot to do with behavior. There are behaviors that have a positive effect, and behaviors that have a negative effect. There is a place to start. There are these five precepts that I try to live by.

First off, I can cause harm to another person. When I do, I find myself in distress. But intention makes a difference. Something done unintentionally will not carry the same weight as something done intentionally. Mistakenly killing a spider is not as cruel as purposely killing a spider. Mistakenly hurting someone's feelings is not as cold as purposely hurting someone's feelings. Mistakenly failing to express compassion is not as selfish as purposely failing to express compassion. When intention becomes my focus, instances where I cause harm can completely disappear.

Secondly, the choices I make each day are important. Interacting with the world is a give-and-take situation. When I am giving, my thoughts can be considerate of others. When I am taking, my thoughts can be considerate of me. When I am taking without taking into account the consideration of others, this could be stealing. I look at it this way: I am making a choice to take something that perhaps I should not be taking. It is best when I abstain from making this choice. I consider it stealing.

Third, much of my practice revolves around relationships. One of the most intense relationships a person can have is a sexual relationship. There can be so much beauty, and there can be much hurt. Within the spiritual discipline that I practice, one's conduct while in a sexual relationship is specifically addressed. Any hurt caused by one's decisions must be avoided. Taking responsibility is key. A sexual relationship brings with it a commitment. It is important for me to accept that at this time, my only commitment is to this transformative process geared toward turning my relationships with all people into a fully rewarding experience for everyone involved. At this moment, I have relationships where sex is not the primary focus.

Fourth, it is necessary to look at honesty again. I express my behaviors, and others experience my behaviors. You only get to know me based upon what I show you. I question if it is possible to really know anybody when there is no truth. A mirror only works when it reflects what is in front of it. I am not in front of you when I lie to you. It is only possible for you to get to know me when I tell you the truth.

The fifth precept is where intoxication comes into play. People are different while intoxicated, and therefore, intoxication requires some clarification. Having one drink could amount to intoxication for some, whereas having one drink could amount to nothing for others. I have a history of drug and alcohol abuse. One drink could amount to intoxication for me. It could alter how I think, feel, and act in a negative way. I then may not deal with situations based on the instincts and behaviors I am learning, but based on an unappealingly altered mind and body. So, I choose not to get intoxicated.

These five precepts of abstaining from harm, not stealing, sexual responsibility, not lying, and avoiding intoxication are what I try to follow. Meditation and spiritual practice only seem to work for me when the life I lead goes in a certain direction. Abiding by the five precepts is an important choice when peace and serenity are the desired result. It is necessary to implement what it is that one needs to do.

CHAPTER 29

THE FIVE HINDRANCES

I CAN SEE where being part of a community has brought me. I am improving at how I look at and treat myself, and I routinely modify my behaviors. However, meditation still plays a big part. I turn to meditation each morning to help my mind and emotions enter a peaceful and calm state. Sometimes it's effortless, but it's not perfect, and it's not guaranteed to always bring about a peaceful and calm state. Sometimes I need to become aware. Sometimes I need see what's here, and then the peace and calm will have a chance to emerge. Sometimes things need to change.

I may wish I had the wealth of others, the success of others, the relationships that others have, or the love that others seem to receive. I may wish I had better clothes, better looks, more money, a better car, or a nicer place to live. I sometimes wish I were friendlier or happier. I tell myself there is nothing wrong with wishing for better things in life, but when I'm sitting alone and quiet, trying to still my mind, I see that wishing for anything at that time is nothing more than a hindrance—the hindrance of covetousness.

Sometimes I wake up in the morning feeling angry and hateful. I don't always know why it happens, but sometimes it's due to the work I have to do that day, an argument I may have had the night before, or even an old memory going back to my childhood. I sit in meditation and see this anger. I am quiet and alone and feeling angry. I see that being angry at that time is nothing more than a hindrance—the hindrance of anger.

I have moments when I am dull or sluggish. There is a lack of enthusiasm and a lack of motivation to meditate. During these times, I'm unable to stay alert and persevere when needed. This is not to be confused with fatigue or sleepiness. Fatigue and sleepiness are remedied with rest and sleep. This sloth, this torpor, is a lack of focus within the mind. The drive is not there, and the mind just wanders away. I sit with a purpose, and this is not the purpose. Sloth and torpor are a hindrance.

At times, there is restlessness and remorse. Restlessness and remorse are experienced as a feeling of regret, nervousness, or worry. When I experience restlessness and remorse, I'm unsettled and anxious. There is grief over something that was done, fear over something that's happening now, or concern over something that might happen in the future. I think about the past, obsess over the present, and try to predict the future. There is no place for this type of thinking during meditation. Restlessness and remorse are a hindrance for me.

I can be uncertain about many things in my life. In fact, it can be hard to imagine *not* being uncertain about things. We live in an unstable, imperfect world. Perhaps uncertainty is the one thing we can be certain of. Sitting in meditation, just seeing and accepting this, could be considered the pinnacle of one's meditative practice. Accepting uncertainty during meditation means there's a possibility of accepting the uncertainty of the world. The moments where I sit and just accept what is here are some of the most peaceful moments I have. Otherwise, there is the hindrance of uncertainty, or in other words, doubt.

These hindrances are meant to be abandoned. When covetousness for the world is abandoned, one can abide with a purified mind released from greed and unwelcome desire. When anger and hatefulness are abandoned, one can abide with a mind free from ill will, anger, and hatred. The mind becomes abundant with compassion for all beings. When sloth and torpor are abandoned, one can abide with a mind full of light, mindful and fully aware. When restlessness and remorse are abandoned, one can abide with a peaceful and unagitated mind. When doubt is abandoned, one abides with a mind that is unperplexed about the wholesome and unwholesome states of the world.

If hindrances are present, there is a reason. One may need to look for this reason, and it might take some time. There should be no annoyance or frustration, though; there can be only patience and persistence. I watch what goes on, and I can see when hindrances are present. The reasons for them will eventually surface, and the choice to abandon what is seen will become available. The path that one takes along the way will determine how easy or hard this is. With a clear mind, I am at my best. I've found that the best way for me to have a clear mind is more meditation. It's time for me to take my meditation to a new level. It's time to start practicing mindfulness of breathing.

CHAPTER 30

MINDFULNESS OF BREATHING, PART ONE

MINDFULNESS OF BREATHING is a meditation practice that's been around for a long time. The Buddha was practicing mindfulness of breathing on the night of his enlightenment. It can be as simple as utilizing the phrase "ever mindful I breathe in, ever mindful I breathe out," but it can also be much more. I will give a detailed explanation of this meditation as I've come to understand it.

First, find a comfortable seated, standing, or lying position. The most common position for meditation is seated upright, not leaning on anything. Meditation, therefore, is often referred to as sitting. You can be seated on the floor, on a cushion, or in a chair; it doesn't matter. Just make sure that you're comfortable.

Sit still, try to relax the mind, and just breathe. Focus on the breath. There doesn't need to be a specific formula or intention to start with. The natural process that the mind will undertake is more than enough.

Thoughts may rush in, or an intolerable itch may develop. Pains, whether sharp, dull, or otherwise, will probably run their typical course of distraction. All this is all right, though thoughts may be especially troubling.

Nonetheless, try to keep your mind on the breath. When the mind wanders, gently bring it back to the breath. Bring your mind back to the breath as often as you have to. Be easy on yourself. It's the same for everyone. Meditation is not always what you would like it to be.

Try to remain still, and breathe. Some people close their eyes while breathing, while some leave their eyes open. Some count their breaths, while others don't. Some people sit indoors, while some sit outside. Some people sit with friends, while others sit alone. Some people set a timer, while others just meditate as long as they can. There really are no steadfast rules. There is only the dedication to just sit and breathe, to try this for a little while. This is meditation.

If initially you can only meditate for five or ten minutes, that's great. Try for as long as you can. Time is not what's important. Eventually, you'll be able to meditate for longer if you choose. Twenty to forty-five minutes is common. It's important not to expect more than what is reasonable. After all, people spend entire lifetimes practicing meditation.

Understand what happens. Your mind is going to wander, your emotions may go crazy, and it all may seem like a big waste of time.

You're going to want to move; you're going to want to

scratch; you're going to want to make that pain go away. It's best to resist these temptations. Perseverance is the antidote for the trials that meditators go through.

Try to focus on one area where you notice the breath. The tip of the nose is often suggested. This is harder than it seems; it may take great awareness to notice the breath at the tip of the nose. However, any point where the breathing is felt can be used. It's important to stick with what you've chosen. There will be rewards. Eventually, the mind will start to grow still. You will know when this happens. At some point, choose to contemplate the words of the Buddha as he talks about mindfulness of breathing:

> Breathing in long, I understand: "I breathe in long"; or breathing out long, I understand: "I breathe out long." Breathing in short, I understand: "I breathe in short"; or breathing out short, I understand: "I breathe out short." I train thus: "I shall breathe in experiencing the whole body [of breath]"; I train thus: "I shall breathe out experiencing the whole body [of breath]." I train thus: "I shall breathe in tranquilizing the bodily formation"; I train thus: "I shall breathe out tranquilizing the bodily formation."
>
> I train thus: "I shall breathe in experiencing rapture"; I train thus: "I shall breathe out experiencing rapture." I train thus: "I shall breathe in experiencing pleasure"; I train thus:

"I shall breathe out experiencing pleasure." I train thus: "I shall breathe in experiencing the mental formation"; I train thus: "I shall breathe out experiencing the mental formation." I train thus: "I shall breathe in tranquilizing the mental formation"; I train thus: "I shall breathe out tranquilizing the mental formation."

I train thus: "I shall breathe in experiencing the mind"; I train thus: "I shall breathe out experiencing the mind." I train thus: "I shall breathe in gladdening the mind"; I train thus: "I shall breathe out gladdening the mind." I train thus: "I shall breathe in concentrating the mind"; I train thus: "I shall breathe out concentrating the mind." I train thus: "I shall breathe in liberating the mind"; I train thus: "I shall breathe out liberating the mind."

I train thus: "I shall breathe in contemplating impermanence"; I train thus: "I shall breathe out contemplating impermanence." I train thus: "I shall breathe in contemplating fading away"; I train thus: "I shall breathe out contemplating fading away." I train thus: "I shall breathe in contemplating cessation"; I train thus: "I shall breathe out contemplating cessation." I train thus: "I shall breathe in contemplating relinquishment"; I train thus: "I shall breathe out contemplating relinquishment."

I breathe and place the Buddha's words in my mind. I seek out the words, contemplate the words, define the words, experience the words, and let my mind do what it's going to do. I devote my time to mindfulness of breathing now. Progress ensues from here.

CHAPTER 31

MEDITATIVE CONCENTRATION

MINDFULNESS OF BREATHING meditation develops concentration, as it keeps one concentrating on the breath. Something can happen. The arising of concentration can bring about a unique state of peace. The ordinary functioning of the body and mind is overcome by a sense of calm and serenity. A wholly positive experience occurs. This is different from what normally occurs. This process has a transformative effect. The results linger after the meditation has ceased. The Buddha called exceptional meditative concentration *jhana*. There are four *jhanas*. I remember the Buddha's description:

> Here, quite secluded from sensual pleasures, secluded from unwholesome states, a person enters upon and abides in the first jhana, which is accompanied by applied and sustained thought, with rapture and pleasure born of seclusion.

Again, with the stilling of applied and sustained thought, a person enters upon and abides in the second jhana, which has self-confidence and singleness of mind without applied and sustained thought, with rapture and pleasure born of concentration.

Again, with the fading away as well of rapture, a person abides in equanimity, and mindful and fully aware, still feeling pleasure with the body, enters upon and abides in the third jhana, on account of which noble ones announce: "This person has a pleasant abiding who has equanimity and is mindful."

Again, with the abandoning of pleasure and pain, and with the previous disappearance of joy and grief, a person enters upon and abides in the fourth jhana, which has neither-pain-nor-pleasure and purity of mindfulness due to equanimity.

The wording of the *jhanas* can be confusing, and it is understandable. The *jhanas* are very deep states. It could be quite difficult to realize what the Buddha is describing. Some people even believe that a realization of the *jhanas* is next to impossible. I see that I have something to work with, though.

The Buddha said, "Having thus abandoned these five hindrances, imperfections of the mind that weaken wisdom, quite secluded from sensual pleasures, secluded from unwholesome states, I entered upon and abided in the first jhana. With the stilling of applied and sustained thought … I entered upon and abided in the second jhana. With the fading away as well of rapture … I entered upon and abided in the third jhana. With the abandoning of pleasure and pain … I entered upon and abided in the fourth jhana."

I try not to focus very hard on the *jhanas*. Perhaps I only focus on the fact that I am without sensual pleasures and unwholesome states when I am sitting alone in meditation, and this brings about a pleasant state. Perhaps I focus on the fact that my thoughts eventually slow down and even stop when I meditate, and this brings about a different kind of pleasant state and a sense of concentration. The pleasant state then starts to subside, and only contentment is left. Once content, I notice that the body and mind can become very peaceful and comfortable.

I notice that when hindrances get in the way, it is harder for me to reach these states of peace and contentment. Their influence creates unrest. Sometimes I try to change that; I try to think my way out of it. When I'm thinking with a mind affected by hindrances, though, the thinking is often ineffective. I've learned this. I've been meditating now for years. Here's what it's been like.

Initially, I was without a community or a teacher, I didn't pay attention to any of the popular spiritual teachings of the day, and I didn't attend any meditation groups. I had only one source of inspiration to turn to: the teachings of the *Majjhima Nikaya*. This had an effect on me. I came up with my own ideas as to what practice would look like for me, and some of it was the truth, and some of it was not.

I started contemplating the *jhanas*. I was intrigued with what they had to say, and I defined them as I saw them at that time. The applied and sustained thought as described in the first jhana were those nagging, unstoppable thoughts coming from my nagging, unstoppable mind. The stilling of applied and sustained thought as described in the second jhana was that amazing time when the nagging, unstoppable thoughts briefly stopped. I believed I was meditating within the first two *jhanas*.

Practice changes over time, though. My view of the *jhanas* is changing. Concentration that is applied and sustained, which then leads to the release of its applied and sustained nature, does not start with the nagging, unstoppable thoughts of a nagging, unstoppable mind. It is the peaceful, undisturbed mind that concentrates and enters into *jhana*. It is the unexcited and calm mind that enters into *jhana*. A person is secluded from sensual pleasures, and a person is secluded from unwholesome states.

I would have insisted that my early abilities were what they were, though. This was important. If someone had convinced me that what I was doing wasn't what I believed it was, I don't know that I would have continued. Much of one's practice can be about getting to know oneself.

The truth may be revealed. I now just try to see my thoughts. I see if they're applied, I see if they're sustained, and I just try to see if I can actually see my thoughts. I see when there are hindrances present, and I realize what I need to do. I need to meditate more.

CHAPTER 32

MINDFULNESS OF BREATHING, PART TWO

THE MINDFULNESS OF breathing meditation continues to grow and expand. There is a teaching known as the four foundations of mindfulness. I work with this teaching.

During meditation, there will be an agreeable, disagreeable, or a neither agreeable nor disagreeable state that exists within the body. *Paying attention to the body is the first foundation of mindfulness.*

There will also be a pleasant, painful, or neither pleasant nor painful feeling that coincides with this state of the body. *Paying attention to feeling is the second foundation of mindfulness.*

The mind is affected by this feeling. *Paying attention to the mind is the third foundation of mindfulness.*

Finally, thoughts occur. *Paying attention to thoughts is the fourth foundation of mindfulness.*

People usually don't pay attention. But when the four foundations of mindfulness are fully understood, changes occur.

The Buddha said, "These four foundations of mindfulness are the bindings for the mind of the noble disciple in order to subdue habits based on the household life, to subdue memories and intentions based on the household life, to subdue distress, fatigue, and fever based on the household life, and in order that one might attain the true way to realize Enlightenment."

I try to incorporate the four foundations of mindfulness into my mindfulness of breathing meditation.

The Buddha explains how one could practice mindfulness of the body:

> On whatever occasion a person, breathing in long, understands: "I breathe in long," or breathing out long, understands: "I breathe out long"; breathing in short, understands: "I breathe in short," or breathing out short, understands: "I breathe out short"; trains thus: "I shall breathe in experiencing the whole body"; trains thus: "I shall breathe out experiencing the whole body"; trains thus: "I shall breathe in tranquillizing the bodily formation"; trains thus: "I shall breathe out tranquillizing the bodily formation."
>
> On that occasion a person abides contemplating the body as a body, ardent, fully aware, and mindful,

having put away covetousness and grief for the world. I say that this is a certain body among the bodies, namely, in-breathing and out-breathing.

He explains how one could practice mindfulness of feeling:

> On whatever occasion a person trains thus: "I shall breathe in experiencing rapture"; trains thus: "I shall breathe out experiencing rapture"; trains thus: "I shall breathe in experiencing pleasure"; trains thus: "I shall breathe out experiencing pleasure"; trains thus: "I shall breathe in experiencing the mental formation"; trains thus: "I shall breathe out experiencing the mental formation"; trains thus: "I shall breathe in tranquillizing the mental formation"; trains thus: "I shall breathe out tranquillizing the mental formation."
>
> On that occasion a person abides contemplating feelings as feelings, ardent, fully aware, and mindful, having put away covetousness and grief for the world. I say that this is a certain feeling among the feelings, namely, giving close attention to in-breathing and out-breathing.

He explains how one could practice mindfulness of the mind:

On whatever occasion a person trains thus: "I shall breathe in experiencing the mind"; trains thus: "I shall breathe out experiencing the mind"; trains thus: "I shall breathe in gladdening the mind"; trains thus: "I shall breathe out gladdening the mind"; train thus: "I shall breathe in concentrating the mind"; trains thus: "I shall breathe out concentrating the mind"; trains thus: "I shall breathe in liberating the mind"; trains thus: "I shall breathe out liberating the mind."

On that occasion a person abides contemplating mind as mind, ardent, fully aware, and mindful, having put away covetousness and grief for the world. I do not say that there is the development of mindfulness of breathing for one who is forgetful, who is not fully aware."

He explains how one could practice mindfulness of mind-objects or thoughts:

On whatever occasion a person trains thus: "I shall breathe in contemplating impermanence"; trains thus: "I shall breathe out contemplating impermanence"; trains thus: "I shall breathe in contemplating fading away"; trains thus: "I shall breathe out contemplating fading away"; trains thus: "I shall breathe in contemplating cessation"; trains thus: "I shall breathe out contemplating cessation"; trains thus: "I shall breathe in contemplating relinquishment"; trains thus: "I shall breathe out contemplating relinquishment."

On that occasion a person abides contemplating mind-objects as mind-objects, ardent, fully aware, and mindful, having put away covetousness and grief for the world. Having seen with wisdom the abandoning of covetousness and grief, they closely look on with equanimity.

When I meditate now I watch the body breathing. I try with enthusiasm and devotion to be aware and mindful of just this moment. There is nothing to like or dislike; no opinions need to be formed. There is no reason to control or change this body. There is no reason to be obsessed with this body. Tranquilize the bodily formation.

Pleasure can arise. I try with enthusiasm and devotion to be aware and mindful of just this moment. There is nothing to like or dislike; no opinions need to be formed. This is pleasure that arises from breathing. It is pleasure like many other pleasures. It is impermanent, so therefore it will end. Practice is meant to show us that which is true. I allow the pleasure to end. Tranquilize the mental formation.

The mind will react. I try with enthusiasm and devotion to be aware and mindful of the mind. What is present will be a pleasant, unpleasant, or neither pleasant nor unpleasant state. There is nothing to like or dislike. I try to pay attention to the mind. There will always be states of mind. No opinions need to be formed. There is just the act of allowing whatever states of mind there are to be what they are. There is peace when there is no worry.

Thoughts will occur. With a worry-free mind, I see that there is the ability to think thoughts that I wish to think. With a calm and peaceful mind, I am able to accept that everything arises, that everything fades, and that it is okay to let go. There is nothing to like or dislike; no opinions need to be formed. I try with enthusiasm and devotion to be aware and mindful of just this moment. I try with enthusiasm and devotion to be aware and mindful that this is equanimity.

CHAPTER 33

MINDFULNESS OF BREATHING, PART THREE

THE MINDFULNESS OF breathing meditation continues to grow and expand. Mindfulness of breathing can bring about the discovery of the seven factors of enlightenment. I look to see how the seven factors of enlightenment could apply during my meditation. But first some preparation is required.

Through meditation, when mindfulness of breathing is practiced daily, I know that I can achieve stability of mind. This meditation is learned and refined over time, and concentration develops.

The body resides in comfort during the meditation. Pleasure is the dominant feeling. I find that the mind can be directed in a certain direction, and acceptance is chosen. There's an ability to think or to not think any thought. Everything that's happening is observed, acknowledged, and enjoyed.

I tend to grow relaxed being in a comfortable body. The body then does what bodies do. The comfort fades away, and the feeling of pleasure leaves. Even though it's undesirable that the feeling of pleasure leaves, it still leaves.

I no longer accept the mind. The mind is being affected by what's going on. It's better when the mind is accepted.

Thoughts arise to try and influence the mind. Stories and ideas of many sorts cause the body to react. My reaction can be pushed in a direction to bring back the feeling of pleasure.

The feeling of pleasure returns, and I again move toward acceptance of the mind. There will be satisfaction if the acceptance returns. The end result will be temporary, though, and I am mindful of this fact. Mindfulness is the first factor of the seven factors of enlightenment.

The seven factors of enlightenment are mindfulness, investigation-of-states, energy, rapture, tranquility, concentration, and equanimity.

There is mindfulness, as in mindfulness of the body, feelings, the mind, and thoughts. I can see the temporary nature of the body, feelings, the mind, and thoughts, and that I am swayed by things of a temporary nature. The complex nature of the truth that motivates me is now revealed.

The enlightenment factor of mindfulness is being developed.

There's inspiration to dig deeper. Any event is looked at with the intention to find what's truly happening.

The impermanent and impersonal nature of everything is repeatedly revealed. The perception that things are otherwise is seen as the cause of much confusion. It's a relief to actually see this.

The enlightenment factor of investigation-of-states is being developed.

The pursuit and the realization of wisdom now dominates what is being done. There's a strong drive to continue. Energy is exerted with sustained determination.

The enlightenment factor of energy is being developed.

The process elicits a deep happiness. It's a happiness that is felt in the body, in the heart, and in the mind. It's an overwhelming happiness. It is rapturous.

The enlightenment factor of rapture is being developed.

The rapture only lasts so long, though; it begins to fade. What remains is a relieved and refreshed body, heart, and mind. When there is no regret regarding the disappearance of the rapture, when there is no desire to bring the rapture back, the new state is superior to the old state. It is tranquil.

The enlightenment factor of tranquility is being developed.

Tranquility leads to concentration. It's concentration that has now become familiar. It's the concentration that occurs when one strives during meditation. This concentration deepens.

The enlightenment factor of concentration is being developed.

Things are changing. Where there once would have

been frustration, there is no frustration. Where there once would have been agitation, there is no agitation. Where there once would have been doubt, there is no doubt. There is peace within the body, with feelings, with the mind, and with thoughts, where there once would not have been peace. Equanimity is prevailing.

The enlightenment factor of equanimity is being developed.

I understand that these seven factors of enlightenment are truly wondrous states. It is here that one will find that what needs to be abandoned and developed, can be abandoned and developed, but the seven factors of enlightenment will only develop when the right conditions are present.

The Buddha said, "Here, people, a person develops the mindfulness enlightenment factor, which is supported by seclusion, dispassion, and cessation, and ripens in relinquishment. A person develops the investigation-of-states enlightenment factor...the energy enlightenment factor...the rapture enlightenment factor...the tranquility enlightenment factor...the concentration enlightenment factor...the equanimity enlightenment factor, which is supported by seclusion, dispassion, and cessation, and ripens in relinquishment."

There is seclusion as in one is without unwholesome states of body and mind. There is dispassion in that one does not want to return to the states that can prevail when one is not secluded. There is cessation in that the energy once promoting these previous states has ceased. Finally, there is relinquishment when you just allow it all to go away.

There are moments when the seven factors of enlightenment fit my meditative experiences very well. There are moments when they do not. It's important to be realistic about what goes on. But one can still dream! I remain inspired.

CHAPTER 34
THE FOUR NOBLE TRUTHS

AT THIS POINT, my understanding and application of Buddhist practice, theory, and philosophy have grown considerably. It can be broken down quite simply, though: it is all based upon the Four Noble Truths.

I love the concept. In fact, I structured the whole middle part of this book guided by the Four Noble Truths. I believe that these truths communicate an important process by which all people can exist in the world. They represent a lifestyle by which everyone could live.

The Buddha said, "At Benares, friends, in the Deer Park at Isipatana the Tathagata, accomplished and fully enlightened, set rolling the matchless Wheel of the Dharma, which cannot be stopped by any recluse or brahmin or god or Mara or Brahma or anyone in the world—that is, the announcing, teaching, describing, establishing, revealing, expounding, and exhibiting of the Four Noble Truths."

The first noble truth states, "This is suffering." I like to define suffering simply as being uncomfortable. See that this suffering comes from within. You're the only one who can suffer. You're not able to suffer for anyone else, and no one else is able to suffer for you.

The second noble truth states, "This is the cause of suffering." See the cause. There can be pain, distress, loss, and other unpleasant things in your life that can cause you to be uncomfortable. One learns from the difficulties of life. The cause of suffering is wanting something to be different than it is, and this wanting comes from within.

The third noble truth states, "This is the end of suffering." This suffering comes to an end from within. Through practice, one can come to believe there is an end to what is within.

The fourth noble truth states, "This is the way leading to the end of suffering." The path to discovering the way leading to the end of suffering, to find the way leading to an understanding of how to change what's within, is the Noble Eightfold Path.

THE NOBLE EIGHTFOLD PATH

The Noble Eightfold Path is the fourth of the Four Noble Truths. The Buddha has this to say about the Four Noble Truths:

And what is suffering? Birth is suffering; aging is suffering; sickness is suffering; death is suffering; sorrow, lamentation, pain, grief, and despair are suffering; not to obtain what one wants is suffering; in short, the five aggregates affected by clinging are suffering. This is called suffering.

And what is the origin of suffering? It is craving, which brings renewal of being, is accompanied by delight and lust, and delights in this and that; that is, craving for sensual pleasures, craving for being, and craving for non-being. This is called the origin of suffering.

And what is the cessation of suffering? It is the remainderless fading away and ceasing, the giving up, relinquishing, letting go, and rejecting of that same craving. This is called the cessation of suffering.

And what is the way leading to the cessation of suffering? It is just this Noble Eightfold Path; that is, right view, right intention, right speech, right action, right livelihood, right mindfulness, and right concentration. This is called the way leading to the cessation of suffering.

After some time and practice, and after some exploration into what it might mean to be the way that a human being could be, the moment is well-suited for me to explain my experience with the Noble Eightfold Path.

CHAPTER 35
RIGHT VIEW

I'VE OFTEN FELT like I don't fit in. It's always been this way. I never liked that it was this way, so I looked for people to show me what to do. Initially, this didn't seem like it would cause a problem. But it is possible to look in an unsuitable direction. What is right for you may be wrong for me, and what is right for me may be wrong for you. I have to tell myself that this is okay, and that I don't have to do what you do, and you don't have to do what I do. I see this as right view.

The Buddha said, "And what, friends, is right view? There is what is given and what is offered and what is sacrificed; there is fruit and result of good and bad actions; there is this world and the other world; there is mother and father; there are beings who are reborn spontaneously; there are in the world good and virtuous recluses and brahmins who have realized for themselves by direct knowledge and declare this world and the other world—this is called right view."

Right view for me is the understanding that everything happening today is happening due to what I am doing. It's the understanding that there are consequences for my actions. It's becoming aware that there is more to this than just what is seen, heard, touched, tasted, smelled, and thought, and that what I am is based upon what I have been taught. Right view is accepting that there is liberation, and that everyone is going to find their own way there.

CHAPTER 36

RIGHT INTENTION

IT STARTS WITH right view. A person with right view gains the ability to know the nature of unimportant things. One dismisses attributes and influences that are unnecessary. Being free from burdens, I am able to engage the world with trained eyes. I can view myself and others with a measure of ease. There can be kindness and compassion behind what I do.

The Buddha said, "And what, friends, is right intention? Intention of renunciation, intention of non-ill will, and intention of non-cruelty - this is called right intention."

CHAPTER 37

RIGHT SPEECH

IT STARTS WITH right view. A person with right view gains the ability to know what it means to be impulsive. Before I speak, I sometimes picture what I'm going to say. I imagine what it would be like to hear the words that I would say being said back to me. I often say that right speech can end up being no speech at all.

I watch to see that what I say isn't a lie. I watch to see that what I say isn't hurtful. I watch to see that what I say isn't mean. I watch to see that what I say isn't nonsense. Right speech often starts with no speech, and then I learn what to say.

The Buddha said, "And what, friends, is right speech? Abstaining from false speech, abstaining from malicious speech, abstaining from harsh speech, and abstaining from idle chatter—this is called right speech."

CHAPTER 38

RIGHT ACTION

IT STARTS WITH right view. A person with right view gains the ability to know how to be careful. Harm can be caused; people hurt each other every day. It's been like this for a long time.

Because I see you as different from me, and I see me as different from you, I end up hurting you, exploiting you, and taking things from of you. People seek liberation, happiness, peace, and a loving, fulfilling life, but they do things that prevent liberation, happiness, peace, and a loving, fulfilling life. Our actions have built this world.

Internal and external lives can be corrupted. I am the one who creates the next scar. I am the one who makes the next choice.

The Buddha said, "And what, friends, is right action? Abstaining from killing living beings, abstaining from taking what is not given, and abstaining from misconduct in sensual pleasures—this is called right action."

CHAPTER 39
RIGHT LIVELIHOOD

IT STARTS WITH right view. I spend a lot of time at work. A person with right view gains the ability to know what it means to do the right kind of work. There is work that harms people, animals, and the planet. This is not the right kind of work; this is not right livelihood.

A person with right view gains the ability to know what it means to behave well when at work. I can be dishonest, rude, mean, and selfish. This is not the right way to behave when at work; this is not right livelihood.

The Buddha said, "And what, friends, is right livelihood? Here a noble disciple, having abandoned wrong livelihood, earns their living by right livelihood—this is called right livelihood."

CHAPTER 40
RIGHT EFFORT

RIGHT EFFORT IS applied to all. Practice requires energy, and it can take time. Many things require patience. I should be easy on myself. Conclusions cannot be drawn until what is supposed to be changed starts to change. It's like this for everyone. Effort is applied to various areas of one's life. I can return as often as is necessary to what I have learned.

The Buddha said, "And what, friends, is right effort? Here a person awakens zeal for the non-arising of unarisen evil unwholesome states, and they make effort, arouse energy, exert their mind, and strive. They awaken zeal for the abandoning of arisen evil unwholesome states, and they make effort, arouse energy, exert their mind, and strive. They awaken zeal for the arising of unarisen wholesome states, and they make effort, arouse energy, exert their mind, and strive. They awaken zeal for the continuance, non-disappearance, strengthening, increase, and fulfilment by development of arisen wholesome states, and they make effort, arouse energy, exert their mind, and strive. This is called right effort."

CHAPTER 41
RIGHT MINDFULNESS

RIGHT MINDFULNESS IS applied to all. Here is the practice of the four foundations of mindfulness evolving. I once saw the processes of life holding me back, and now I see the processes of life moving me forward.

The Buddha said, "And what, friends, is right mindfulness? Here a person abides contemplating the body as a body, ardent, fully aware, and mindful, having put away covetousness and grief for the world. They abide contemplating feelings as feelings, ardent, fully aware, and mindful, having put away covetousness and grief for the world. They abide contemplating mind as mind, ardent, fully aware, and mindful, having put away covetousness and grief for the world. They abide contemplating mind-objects as mind-objects, ardent, fully aware, and mindful, having put away covetousness and grief for the world. This is called right mindfulness."

CHAPTER 42

RIGHT CONCENTRATION

CONCENTRATION IS DEEPENING. Concentration that once was difficult is no longer difficult. Right concentration can occur when the Noble Eightfold Path is a part of one's life.

The Buddha said, "What is noble right concentration with its supports and its requisites, that is, right view, right intention, right speech, right action, right livelihood, right effort, and right mindfulness? Unification of mind equipped with these seven factors is called noble right concentration with its supports and its requisites."

My thoughts, words, and actions are aligning, unlike before. Instead of clinging, there is release of this world. It's understood how the end of suffering could occur. It's understood how the peace and serenity that I have been diligently striving for could be possible.

The Buddha said, "And what, friends, is right concentration? Here, quite secluded from sensual pleasures, secluded from unwholesome states, a person enters upon and abides in the first jhana, which is accompanied by applied and sustained thought, with rapture and pleasure born of seclusion. With the stilling of applied and sustained thought, they enter upon and abide in the second jhana, which has self-confidence and singleness of mind without applied and sustained thought, with rapture and pleasure born of concentration. With the fading away as well of rapture, they abide in equanimity, and mindful and fully aware, still feeling pleasure with the body, they enter upon and abide in the third jhana, on account of which noble ones announce: 'This person has a pleasant abiding who has equanimity and is mindful.' With the abandoning of pleasure and pain, and with the previous disappearance of joy and grief, they enter upon and abides in the fourth jhana, which has neither-pain-nor-pleasure and purity of mindfulness due to equanimity. This is called right concentration."

BOOK 3
THE INNERMORE

THE TRANSITION

It is poetry for you; it seems real to me. It is symbolic for you; it's like a dream to me.

CHAPTER 43
INTRODUCTION

AT THE END of book two, I must continue. It's what I will do, because the past is still faceless, the craving remains ageless, and this work is yet nameless. I might want things to be another way, but the words are still making it to the paper.

I'm trying to get a point across. We're all trying to make a point. In the end, nothing important is going to be said, though. This ultimately is the point, but I am a writer.

It's time to change the flavor; it's time to dull the razor. Something will come from nothing.

You still will read whatever you want to read. Pay attention to how you feel; it is how you feel, and it won't remain, but see what's left behind. This is what gets written, and this is what gets read.

CHAPTER 44

THE JOURNEY

I CAN FEEL the dirt in my bones, the ocean is in my blood, and moonlight fills my mind. Words such as these come from me now. Years of Buddhist practice can change a person.

For some time now, I've been spending time solely with Buddhist meditators. It has brought me to this current state. I've looked internally at how I feel, and have gained some peace with how I feel. I've looked externally at how I behave, and have improved how I behave. I've deepened my Buddhist studies, and have started to understand my Buddhist studies, all whilst among my Buddhist friends. It makes sense that this is how it is.

A struggle with a person is a solution found in me, a behavior that is offensive becomes a change for those to see, a teaching that is confusing is a conversation for us all, and a meditation that is challenging on my lone shoulders need not fall. The times have improved, as one would expect that they should. The people have shown that their will is to be good.

I love what I do with my friends. We sit in our apartments, eat great takeout food, meditate with each other, and discuss our many moods. We ride our bicycles to the movies, visit exotic places, attend the greatest art openings, and have grand celebrations. We enjoy the breeze along the waterfront, and shop in the coolest stores. We walk endlessly down the streets, and ride the subway near and far. I love the lifestyle that New York City has to offer. I want to live in New York, so I am moving here. My friends are starting to change, though. Things always seem to change.

I've grown unsettled. Things always seem to grow unsettled. My friends don't believe me anymore. They say it is impossible, what I do. The work I do, my striving, the changes, all seem unlikely—but no one here knows the junkie I used to be. I can understand. It doesn't make sense that the person I once was is the person that I am today. Logic doesn't explain me, and the friends that I have, as great as they are, have become just too logical for me. I need to find the illogical ones. I need to find the ones who live the impossible. I'm going to go dancing, and things will never be the same.

CHAPTER 45

IMAGINE

IMAGINE DANCING. IMAGINE dancing until you drop. Imagine letting go of all concerns about how you look, how you feel, or even how you smell.

Dancing can be primal and pure. It's one of the earliest forms of honest, unfiltered expression that we know of. For thousands of years, groups of dust-covered humans have danced in the moonlight, danced around a fire, danced until they fell in love. See the image that this creates.

One might question these things that are not controlled. People are not meant to be controlled. We are meant to be free. We are born of the spirit.

CHAPTER 46

THE DANCE

I SEE THE dance like this. There's a room, and it's empty. The room always starts out empty. Everyone shows up, but no one is warm. This is the cold time, the uncertain time, the time to look around. The music is slow, the music is peaceful, but it calls us to move.

I feel the earth, and I spin in circles until I'm warm, until everybody else is warm, and then I arrive. I see everyone else, and everyone else is arriving, and we start to flow. We're new to this stream of life, and everything is being taken care of.

Things can change, though. The music is starting to pick up. It's time to try and control this life. It's time to plan, it's time to prepare, it's time to make things secure. I feel the beat, and I will move to the beat, and this gives me ideas. I'll master the weather when I put on a coat, I'll slow down time as I run very fast, and I'll live my life once I learn how.

I see that my ideas work for just so long, though. The weather's now hot, there's too much time, and this is the reality. As a kid, I used to hear the ocean in a shell, see lightning in a bug, and watch the stars fall. The ocean doesn't fit in a shell, though, lightning doesn't come from a bug, and the stars don't really fall. My eyes are opening, and the roles are changing. I see there is no control. The music's getting louder now. The music's getting crazy, and here comes the chaos.

Let there be chaos. Dance, scream, fall down, and love. It is unknown until it's tried. It's so good this way. The cloth will unravel, the flood is going to force the dam, but the light will shine beyond the curtain. Release this uncertainty; don't let it stay inside. Express it all, and just let it all go. Free the dancer, and dance the dance, as the dance is you. My whole life, I missed this. The mirror kept my face from being seen. The mirror is broken now, though, and I just lost all the pieces. However, I can still breathe, and it will be okay. The music will eventually slow down.

The music is slowing down now, and everyone is finding themselves in a new place. I'm with everyone, and we're sweating and sliding together. We now know who we are. We're too tired for choices, so we're just here. We're graceful, we're moving, and there is meaning. I am beautiful as you are beautiful, but I am flawed as you are flawed, and I am great as you are great, but we are in awe as we are no more. We're seeing each other for the first and final time, because it's all about to end. We're about to become bones.

The time has come to breathe once more; the time is now for us to be still. We've never felt this way before; until again we meet, and then again we will. We're peaceful, and look at how we got here. We danced here. We just danced the 5Rhythms.

CHAPTER 47

GABRIELLE ROTH'S 5RHYTHMS

I'VE BEEN LIVING in New York City for some time now, and I now attend 5Rhythms dance classes. 5Rhythms dance classes in New York City are a special kind of place. New York has perhaps the greatest of everything, so it makes sense that it would have the greatest dance classes. It's a big claim to make, and a big claim to try to describe.

I find myself walking down a long hallway. On either side of the hallway, there are large windows peering into the different dance studios. There are jazz dancers in the studios, ballet dancers, modern free-form dancers, and classical, choreographed, well-structured types of dancers. To navigate this hallway is a bit of a challenge. There are people everywhere, stretching, standing, running, sitting, talking, eating organic food, and drinking electrolyte-infused drinks.

There are people everywhere in leotards, costumes, sweats, shorts, lots of clothes, and very little clothes. There are people so very fit, they look like chiseled sculptures. There are people not so very fit who look like determined warriors. Everyone is welcome here. Everybody has their place. We are all dancers. I reach the end of the hallway, and I see my group.

We are a mix of everything: young, old, professional, not professional, amateur dancers, great dancers, and those dancing for the first time. There are close to one hundred of us. Our dance classes tend to be quite large. We talk, mingle, stretch, eat organic food, and drink electrolyte-infused drinks. We are preparing to go into the room. We have our own dance studio for the day.

In the room, the 5Rhythms dance begins. First, there is a style of dance consisting of flowing circular movements. There then is a style of dance consisting of sharp, defined movements. Then a somewhat chaotic style of dance consisting of just about any kind of movement you wish to make. Next, there is a style of dance consisting of relaxed, smooth, and even bouncy kinds of movements. Finally, there is a stillness at the end where it all just slows down, and eventually stops. The 5Rhythms are flowing, staccato, chaos, lyrical, and stillness. It is the music that dictates where you go. The music sings the 5Rhythms. The music belts out the 5Rhythms sound, and you just follow it wherever it takes you. I sometimes can't believe where it takes me. It is the illogical that I've been looking for.

My friend is dancing true and hard, and light beams spring from her hands. I am dancing with my spirit, and I am alone where I stand. My friend is dancing with her ancestors, and I am invited to join in. I am dancing with her ancestors, and she and I become one within.

This is the impossible that I felt was true. I cannot fault the others for not being here too. Unless you experience the experience, it is not true for you.

I am going to leave the logical ones right where they stand. I am going to dance with the illogical ones. I belong with those who dance!

My New York City adventure is well on its way. Now I hang with some of the hippest people I've ever known. Artists, musicians, painters, sculptors, photographers, and professional dancers are now my friends, and there are a lot of us. We normally make reservations that are in the double digits. This is a happy time.

I should just sit back and live this life now. It seems like this is the place where one would want to arrive. I would think that my mind would be content here. This is not the case. I feel that I must go deeper; I must be the one they call the eternal seeker. I'm not able to just leave things alone. It's time to dig right in.

CHAPTER 48

REVELATION

I NOW CLEARLY see that it is our minds that create this world. It can be hard to believe. People will argue that the world exists with or without a mind. We all have a mind, so we're all free to think whatever we want to think. I'm learning a lot.

Look at how I used to be. I used to just walk all over the place. This was especially true late at night. Everything changes late at night. The sidewalks are empty, and the houses are dark. The lights are in the sky. I've experienced the magic with little distraction, but I never knew that I did.

The water flowed through the tunnels, the trees grew among the poles, and the ground was hard with concrete and tar. I journeyed through this as I made my way home. I then put a book on the shelf, and the carpenter showed me her skills, the plumber handed me a glass of water, and the farmer fed me cereal. This makes me grow unnerved; I thought I was alone. It's magic, or its lunacy. There can be lunacy.

They tell me that fire hydrants, garbage cans, and lampposts are made of the same stuff that I'm made of. They say the wind that blows down Broadway is the wind that once blew in the pirate's sail. They tell me that the water my cat drinks is the water that someone once cried.

We're affected by all of this. It's difficult when it is unknown. All I can do is dance. I can't stop the wind, and I can't help but cry.

Just dance hard enough, just dance fast enough, and you'll see just how fragile this body is. You'll see how fragile the people are. Be kind to the people. We're all the same. We want to be happy in this life. See that we experience life everywhere we go, and that where we go can be quite amazing.

WISDOM

Penetrate through to what is real. Feel for the depth of night; the dark doesn't see the light. We are all contained within a body. This is something that should be obvious, but perhaps it is the obviousness of it all that blinds us to what could be seen.

CHAPTER 49
EARTH

UNDERSTAND THAT THE earth is here for us to trust and rely on. We are held in place by the ground beneath our feet. Imagine there is release from the bond. It must feel great.

Run, breathe in the air, dive in the river, jump, and fly along. This is freedom. I wish that freedom was always true, and that everyone would just close their eyes and let me be free. Freedom is true when there is only a moment, but I always seem to get caught.

I can still try to go somewhere, though, and it might be time to go somewhere. It is okay to look back. The journey is better when there is someplace to return to. Our skin, our bones, and our muscles do like to stay put. I'm going to allow everything to stay put today.

Realize that we are alive, and contained in this vessel, and that this vessel can be knocked over. Sand flows as we flow. The dust blows as we blow. Our bodies go as everything must go. See that there are the parts of this body that are the same as the parts of this earth. Let the earth and the body be as they will be.

CHAPTER 50
FIRE

EVERYTHING WILL EVENTUALLY catch on fire, though. Fire clarifies. See what's undefined. I'm alive on the inside; I live on the outside; the fire won't let me hide. It lights my way.

I want people to see me, and I know it will change them. I do care, but some things can't be avoided. My heart generates heat. You can feel it when I hug you.

I think I just made you warm.

You can hug me too. Everyone would like to share themselves. We all need to be seen. You can show me what you love. You aren't being selfish. It's not one-sided.

Have no fear to let go—or just have your fear, and still let go. I want what you will offer. I will let you share the covers.

Fire burns the paper, fire burns the wood, fire makes things equal, but we are people. Be sure of what you are, be sure of what you do, and just let the fire burn as it burns. You won't get hurt. The fire is in you, and it is in me too.

CHAPTER 51

WATER

FIRE CHANGES WHEN it rains. The rain doesn't care that I'm not prepared, though. My bike has no fenders, the ground soaks my shoes, and my lighter won't light.

People are fallible. My bike is actually a hunk of junk, these shoes really don't fit, and I don't have anything to ignite. I might be missing many things. I can try to understand what it means.

I look for you, and I don't see you. I can't touch what I can't reach. You call to me, but I am hidden. I eat my meal alone. Your scent is still unknown.

Life can be unpredictable. There can be nothing we can do to change things, but when I see a person scream on the subway, I still look in disbelief. Sometimes people know more than me. What I hold inside eats me alive.

I can turn to the water to see what to do. Shake with vibration, and splash when dropped, freeze in the freezer, and boil when hot. The water won't resist; it knows how to exist.

Perhaps I'll just let life knock, and I'll laugh, and I'll jump, and I'll dance right through. It's my turn now. I'm going to take a chance; this I won't miss. I will find my voice, and I will scream, "Yes!"

CHAPTER 52

AIR

I'M GOING TO fly now, as the lightning flies through the sky. Breathe in what you like, and breathe out the fright. I don't drink for days, I don't eat for weeks, I don't breathe for minutes, and I die. When I was a child, I used to fly kites.

My dad bought me a really nice kite once. It was made of cloth, it had a beautiful tail, and it came with a very long ball of string. It went higher than any of the other kites in the park. It would fly across the baseball field, across the soccer field, and out over the road. I loved watching it fly over the road. It was so far away.

One time the string broke, and I ran. I ran as fast as I could across the baseball field, across the soccer field, and out into the road. The kite was down. It had broken its back. What flies is so beautiful, and what flies is so fragile.

I'm no longer a child now. I look both ways when I cross the street. Someone has to cross the street, and I know how it feels to fall. I love that I know.

Watch the birds as they fly, dive, and twirl. Their wings carry them high, the wind carries them higher, and I know that they don't care. They know what to do, but we need to be mindful of the wind. We're meant to walk on two feet, but we too love to fly.

CHAPTER 53

SPACE

IT'S FUN TO move into the empty space. This space is now with me. It's fun to move out of the empty space. This space is now without me. Something just happened. Perhaps the space disappeared, and then reappeared. Something must happen.

Watch the trees as they blow in the wind. Their leaves move into the empty space. This space is now with the leaves. Their leaves move out of the empty space. This space is now without the leaves. Things are in one place, and then they are in another place. Everything actually could be in just one place.

This empty space is inside of us. Contemplate what this could mean. When we dance our dance, our dance is one; when we love our love, our love is one; our empty spaces are now just one. It's quite an idea, and some ideas matter. I move with you, and now my space is in you. You move with me, and now your space is in me. This is amazing, but just let it all go. I spend my time thinking of crazy things.

I wonder if I see the world like other people do. Maybe it's that I see a world that most people just do not see. I'll feel better if I think that I'm not alone. Space is emptiness, as I like to see it, and space as emptiness is here if you believe it.

Just sit still, and be still. Breathe in, and breathe out. Watch what you see. Our bodies will rise and fall. The feelings will rise and fall. The mind will rise and fall. See how obsessed you become, see how free you become. Just like that, there is the rise and the fall of everything.

Understand that there can be no worries, no stories, no future, and no past, but just peace. This is emptiness born of this moment. This is peace. This is space. This is our stillness.

CHAPTER 54

ME

IT'S ONLY WHEN I find the stillness that I realize that stillness is not so still. It's in the stillness that I notice everything moving. I have nothing to see, hear, touch, taste, smell, or even think about, but there is so much going on. This makes no sense. I think it's not supposed to make sense. The sun and the moon are shining together. I wonder what this is.

I realize that I'm trying to understand what's within. I don't think that I yet understand. My life is still so daunting. I go to work, I spend time with my group of friends, I meditate, I dance, I read a lot, and I write. Sometimes I get to ride my bike.

Keep going. When one finds what more there is to be discovered, there is clarity and joy. There's a sense that there is little need for anything else. There is dispassion toward the things that deceive. The mind starts to feel free. It can look at itself perhaps for the first time, but we are human beings, and human beings can be comfortable when there is bias. I love you, but I hate you, and I just don't care about the rest of you. We tend to judge. Our intentions toward each other can be impure.

Purity does exist, though. I can see you for what you really are, and I can see me for what I really am. There is no need to cling to you, or to reject you, or to ignore you. There is no need to dismiss that you are here. I can love you, and I can love me, and I love that we are here. I cannot love you, and I cannot love me, and I don't love that we are here. I see that both of us aren't really here after all. Let's do this together. The word *love* is no longer ruined.

See what causes everything. An experience is felt as pleasant in the moment, an experience is felt as painful in the moment, and an experience is felt as neither pleasant nor painful in the moment. The moment is then over, and the feeling is then over, but we don't let it be over. We think about the pleasant moment, we think about the painful moment, and we think about the moment that is neither pleasant nor painful. We give the past features, and we construct our futures. We're obsessive creatures.

It's only when we know what we do that one begins to understand. I created all of this. The good, the bad, the ecstasy, the love, the worry, and the beauty all come from me. The mind never stops. It has what it has, it does what it does, and I can lose track.

The girl whom I once loved, I no longer love, my mom has long since passed, my first meditation has already happened, and I've danced my best dance. I can see why I feel the way I do. I can see why I think the way I do. I can see why I act the way I do. I see my influences, and I create my influences.

I woke up at 4:00 a.m. today, I drank tea, I studied, and I meditated. It's never stopped. I settle the mind and body. I let yesterday go. I don't know what today will be, and I am still. This is what happens in the morning. It's peaceful. Life can be otherwise for me, and then the morning is not the same, but I no longer dance alone. I dance with you, and I know that when I dance, I become what I dance. This I can understand.

THE DEPTHS

CHAPTER 55

REALITY

MY MIND IS starting to question things, though. I am experiencing the greatest joy dancing with my friends. I am in constant amazement that I actually am a dancer. Running around New York City with a bunch of dancers just seems too cool for me to do. It's not that I am denying that this is true. I am seeing that the Buddhist practice brought this about, and I wonder if there's more, so I'm going back for more. I'm going back to the meditation class.

This is still a popular class. A lot of people still attend. The teacher is talking about focus, and practice, and treating yourself well, and treating others well, and it all probably sounds good to most people. I am listening. He is stating the facts and the studies. He is pointing to the applications, the benefits, and the improvements that one could make to one's life. The class has not changed. It still makes too much sense.

After class, a woman puts on her shoes and coat, and she leaves. A couple of people are chatting in the corner. A man finishes a bottle of water, throws out the bottle, and he leaves. Three people leave together. A couple more people are chatting. The teacher is cleaning up his area. I talk to some friends, and they are happy to see me. They talk about how good the class was, and I just nod. I don't know why I don't say that I really didn't like anything about it. I lace up my sneakers, grab my bicycle helmet, and walk out the door.

I ride my bike down the street, and I look up at the sky. It's a clear sky, and the stars are out. The temperature is mild. I ride under a massive bridge. I always love riding under massive bridges. I ride past a line of cars that are not moving because other cars are in their way. I always love riding past a line of cars that are not moving because other cars are in their way. I pedal furiously in low gear just to make it up a hill. I pedal furiously in high gear just to speed down the other side of the hill. I ride through the park. I see the drum circle drummers pounding perfectly. A band is playing music. There are a lot of people walking, and lots of dogs barking, and a bunch of kids playing. There is me riding my bicycle across Brooklyn on a night when the stars are out. I love riding my bicycle across Brooklyn on a night when the stars are out.

I see it now. I felt disappointment as I left the meditation class, but then I experienced the night. I experienced the bridge. I experienced the cars. I rode hard to try and experience me. The drummers made me bounce, the band made me sing, the people made me smile, and by the end of the night, everything was different.

Life can be deceiving. There's unhappiness, and there's the happiness that I seek, and there can be uncertainty about how to actually get there. But the things that truly make me happy can be right in front of my eyes.

I can try to picture it. There is disappointment, and I strive for ecstasy; there is pain, and I must have relief; there is heartbreak, and I crave to try again. I cry, and then I laugh; I scream, and then I'm silent; I smash my hand, and then I lick the wound. Life can be seen as an equation that's meant to be balanced. People will agree that balance is a good idea.

It may never end, though. We're trapped, and no one knows. It takes a subtle eye to see until there's nothing left to see. We won't need a subtle eye then. The voices cry out loud and clear. It's no longer working. I'm giving up on this meditation class.

I still ride my bike across Brooklyn, though. I notice the cars, the big, beautiful bridges, and the stars in the sky. I notice all the people, and I admit to myself that there is no equation to be balanced. There are only those of us who will stay put, and those of us who look for more. Everyone can choose their future, and I'm starting to learn what that looks like for me.

CHAPTER 56

MYSTERY

I'D LIKE TO be able to discuss what this is, but this is about experience. The poet dies without perfecting the craft. The song has yet to be written; the picture was never taken; the painting is still unpainted. The truth is hidden, and this is not the proper place. The world rejects what is misunderstood. The beautiful still will appear, though, but the beautiful doesn't look the way that is expected. It's not found in the world. We all are born here, and we all have to function here, but we don't have to exist here. Through practice, one could see.

The pleasure you feel you need not suppress, the pain you feel could hurt much less, the joy you feel will have no best, and the grief you feel can come to rest.

One can abandon the world. This is what is misunderstood. People normally don't abandon the world, and when we are told to abandon the world, we either reject the idea, or we try to fulfill the idea, and none of it works.

The methods used in the world work only for their own purposes. There is confusion, but there is another way. Look this way.

Here I see groups of monks in temples. Incense burns, drums bang, horns blare, and the monks are chanting. The walls are decorated. There are elaborate colored paintings of amazing beings smiling and laughing. There's smoke, and there's color, and glitter, and shiny, soft, hard, and beautiful things. The horns are lunatic animals, the drums make no sense, and I have no idea what the monks are chanting, but they just don't stop.

I dance all over the room. I'm up in the air, skipping and jumping. There's joy in all this madness. My friends are here, and we are in love. We dance together, and we are friends together, and we love together. It all gets to be enough. We stop, we drip, we pant, and we breathe. I look around with my hands on my hips. The teacher looks out and knows what she's done. We're both in ecstasy, smiling and sweating.

I didn't just arrive at this place. It took a lot for me to get here. The monks I see and the dance I dance are one and the same. There are many forms, and I enter into the form of stillness. I experience peace and purity of mind here. Things are not pleasurable and things are not painful here. Identity serves no purpose here. Differences fade away. I can see the monks, and I can dance the dance, and there is nothing to cling to.

I'm abiding in unknown states, and I'm witnessing all of it. I wish I could tell you, but I can only share with you.

Please understand why. Please understand what I'm trying to do. Please understand what I'm trying to say. There is mystery, but this mystery is nothing. It has no color, no shape, no direction, and it takes up no space. Mystery is in the moment when you look in wonder and see that this is actually happening.

Pleasure is embraced with the greatest enthusiasm because there is no fear of the pleasure going away. You're in the middle of a most joyful place, knowing that you really are here, and you are being all yes.

Pain is engaged with all of its nastiness because you realize that something brought you here. You're in the middle of a most messed-up place, knowing that you really are here, and you are being just this.

Try to see what's going on. Please, it's not about what we've done. Walk with me, and live this with me. I can only speculate why all this is happening. I see something when I look in your eyes, though. I'm here with you, and I feel no fear. Let go and abide with me in the mystery.

CHAPTER 57

INFINITE PLACES

THE MYSTERY IS all around us now, and a door reveals that there are infinite places. The infinite places are different. Infinite places have no form. As soon as something assumes a form, it tends to stay that way. Infinite places can be anything, anywhere, at any time.

A person develops what they need to. Behaviors are addressed, restraints are abandoned, thoughts are released, and one lets go. Abide in mystical states. The practice will dive deep and burst forth.

Now walk down the street, being completely immersed. See that all people are people, as you too are a person; see that everything alive is alive, as you too are alive; see that everything dead is dead, as you too will be dead. See what it feels like to be on the street, but understand that the street is often misunderstood. We can harm ourselves and others. We can harm the world. If a person is going to experience peace of mind, there will be the wisdom of the street.

See that it is the tragedy of our selfishness that drives the seeker. I never knew why I felt the way I did. My dad cut down the trees, and I hated him for it, but then I killed the bees for the fun of it. I was so confused. I never knew the rules. So, I sought why, and found there is room within, there is breath within, and there is emptiness within. It is a place undefined. I can draw one thousand pictures and still never capture what could be captured. I don't know what anything is, and I can't think about it, but I've learned that nothing is something. Now this is what I call meditation.

It is the deep place. Space is seen to go on forever, the mind encompasses an endless expanse, the immense void is fully experienced, and the perception that one has of any and all things serves no purpose. The impossible becomes the possible for just this moment. Don't try and make this moment longer than it's supposed to be. It is truly vital knowledge to know how long a moment is supposed to be.

One will need to stay calm when the circumstances become too much, though. We are fearful animals. Our bodies will react when we are amongst the depths, and the mind will search for a solution, for an escape, but there is no solution, and there is no escape. We're here because of a place we've already been. This is conditioned. Let it be. It's going to go where it needs to go.

These deep moments, shallow moments, waking moments, sleeping moments, engaged moments, and disengaged moments all have a beginning, a time, and an end. There will be no doubt when a nail is through the wood and a hammer is in the hand. The question of "why" is answered with a definitive "I did this."

When I don't feel love, though, there is no hammer. When I do feel love, there is no hammer. I practice to find what is elusive. Seek the elusive, and the obvious will be easy. Watch the monk as he smiles softly. Watch the dancer as she dances beautifully. Some people have already found it.

I found a Zen priest today. I questioned him on what happens. I questioned him on why I continue as I do. "I can't explain what goes on with me, the teacher doesn't teach this to me, the answer falls short of reaching me. I keep trying, with nothing to find." I knew the Zen priest would know what to say. I wanted to join him. I wanted to study with him. I wanted to practice like him. He listened, he was looking at me, and he was smiling. I should have done this a long time ago. This man is so wise. He has an answer. "Don't worry; I'm sure that I too will let you down."

I am alone today. There is no priest, and no one knows that I am here. Pretty soon I'm going to have a cup of coffee. I think about this as I sit under a tree. There is no coffee until I actually have it, though. This is what happens. This is all that needs to happen.

CHAPTER 58
BEING NON-BEING

I'M SITTING BY myself in my room today. I have a one-of-a-kind, custom-built art deco chair that I sit in. It's one of the few possessions that I still carry around. I've gotten rid of most everything else. I have a bicycle, some clothes, a few decorations for the wall, some Buddhas, a backpack, and a bamboo plant. I have a screwdriver, a pair of pliers, a fan for the window, a tent, and a sleeping bag. I have a handful of random books, a copy of the *Majjhima Nikaya*, and a suitcase. I have a basket of important paperwork, a beach bag, beach towels, suntan lotion, and another basket with some random stuff that I forget about. I forget about some stuff. I have an iPhone, a television, and a reading lamp. That's about it. It's going to take two or three people maybe one or two trips to get rid of everything that was mine when I die. I'm comfortable in this place. The mind wonders if I'm safe, though. It's one of the mind's jobs. It can be my only source of anxiety when left unchecked. The inexperienced mind can be distracted by what it believes.

Another decoration fell off my wall today. It's the fourth thing to fall off the wall. I've just been leaving everything on the floor. There's a mandala that's still up, the face of a deity from Tibet, a chart of the chakras, and the cross from my mom's coffin. It's interesting to see what remains. I like it when I don't question everything. I like it when I don't try and fix everything. I'm too busy right now exploring an extremely faraway state. This body is numb, and then vibration, and then gone. Thoughts are floating banners. Blinking lights gesture and disappear. All is good because impermanence is real. My vision is penetrating, and ecstasy is found.

I'm believing for the first time ever that there is nothing else going on. I'm believing for the first time ever that nothing else matters. For just this moment, the world and everything that goes along with the world is not important. It becomes clear only when I look back. I emerge from the state that I'm in, and I breathe.

I notice that my wall is nearly bare. I'm going to leave the wall this way. If the mandalas and chakras fell off the wall, I would leave it this way. If the crosses and faces fell off the wall, I would leave it this way. It all seems so uneventful since all these events pertain to the world, and the true reality is showing itself. This is my experience.

It takes a lot of imagination. I know. I live by imagination. Leave this place and come back here again. If something is different, then it was worth the effort.

CHAPTER 59
IT HAS BEEN DONE

LIFE IS THIS way now. I'm fully engulfed, but the world is trying to invade what I am. It's not the world's fault, what it does. The world is acting the way it's supposed to, but I'm now barely recognized. Presence is the guardian of the being. I try to understand what this means.

When you're present, the effect that the past is having on you is well known, the concerns that you have about the future are well known, and the realization that neither the past nor the future has to have influence on you is well known.

There's an ability to see rise and fall. This is not where you declare that I'm in this moment, I'm supposed to be in this moment, or I can't believe that I'm not in this moment. This is where a person accepts that this is exactly how this is in this moment. Impermanence, which could be a cause of much discomfort, could also be a cause of much joy, and the magic begins.

I enjoy what's going on. I like to meditate with the rise of the sun, the sound of the drummers as they drum as one, and the touch of my love when we dance until done. I'm going to go as deep as I can. There is no holding back, only release. I'm allowing this to be as great as it could be. I find no reason not to. It's only painful when it ends, and I already know that it's going to end.

I accept what's going on. I don't like the times when I feel upset, the sway of the people who cause me regret, and the places I go with unclear intent. I look at what I know. When mindfulness is undeveloped, there will be attachment to what does not stay. Everything will end, though. There is one pleasant thing about unpleasant things: unpleasant things are pleasant when they end.

I understand what's going on. I sit and just stare as we drive down the road, the water feels warm after it first feels cold, and the song will play until it finally gets old. It's time to acknowledge the truth. I either just let things be as they are, or I try to make things be as I would like them to be. The mind rushes to find the pleasure, and the mind runs from the pain. There are the times when there is neither pleasure nor pain. There is nothing that I need to do.

I'm waiting for things to settle down now. I've got to learn it sooner or later. It may happen in the next minute, by the next day, before next year, or it will happen when I die. I don't always know if I have what it takes. This is not the point. If I were to ask my mom, she would tell me to smile as I die. This is the point. Smile as I die, and everything will subside.

PIVOT

CHAPTER 60
AYAHUASCA

A FRIEND OF mine from the dance class just invited me to do ayahuasca. Being a recovering drug addict, I am looking at this invitation with some skepticism. Ayahuasca is considered by many to be not just some hallucinogenic drug, though. It's not meant to be something you just do for fun. Ayahuasca is meant to be done as part of a ritualistic ceremony presided over by an experienced shaman. The ceremonies are known to have amazing healing effects. They can produce mind-blowing experiences that can ultimately leave people transformed. I did my research, and I'm going to do ayahuasca with my friend.

We arrive at the farm in New Jersey, where the ayahuasca ceremony is about to begin, and we greet the other people we are going to be in ceremony with. They seem like very nice people. We are brought to the ceremonial room. It's set up with Tibetan prayer flags, Native American sculptures, flowers, and beautiful psychedelic pictures on the wall.

There is a circle of cushions for us to sit on, a fireplace in the corner, various trinkets brought by the people in the ceremony, drums, a flute, and the shaman's altar set up in the middle of it all. It's an attractive setup. We sit down in the room and wait for the shaman.

The shaman arrives. She is dressed in a beautiful long red dress and has a look of combined confidence and calm that immediately puts me at ease. She has clearly done this before. The shaman chats with us for a few minutes, then settles down near her altar. She begins chanting, singing, playing the drums, and playing the flute. She burns sage, blows tobacco smoke around the room, dances, and speaks welcoming words meant to open the ceremony.

This is truly different. It feels very ancient. I feel as if I'm in another time, another era—a place other than a farm in New Jersey. I love this. I've searched for the impossible people. These seem like the truly impossible people.

We sit in a circle, not speaking. We're just listening to the shaman's chants and songs. I stare out into the room and grow very quiet.

The time eventually comes for us to take the ayahuasca. The shaman gives us the ayahuasca drink, and we sit, and we wait. Hours pass by. I can't believe the patience that everyone exhibits. The fireplace is lit and crackling away. The smell of sage is everywhere. The shaman quietly chants. I notice my eyes growing heavy. It's the middle of the night now, and I'm growing tired. I don't know that I can stay awake. I decide I'm going to just lay back on my cushion now and relax.

I can't fall asleep. I want to fall asleep, but there's a spot in the center of my vision when I close my eyes. I don't know what it is, but I want it to stop. The spot is racing towards me. I open my eyes, and it goes away. I close my eyes, and it returns. I want to fall asleep, but there's this spot; but I'm too tired, so I just let it go; and now I am flying.

I am flying through long tunnels of spinning, wonderfully colored shapes of triangles and squares and circles. Everything is silvery, shining, and spinning with colors unimaginable. I turn left; I turn right. I can go anywhere that I'd like to go. Walls of color dissolve in front of me. Walls of color form behind me. I turn around, and the walls open up. I go this way. I turn around again, and the walls open up. I go this way.

My body is shaking. The shaman is chanting. A person is singing. The fire is crackling. This is amazing. I don't know that I ever want to leave this place.

It seems like hours have passed since I've entered these tunnels, and now I can feel my heartbeat. I hear my heartbeat. It's so very loud. My heartbeat seems to fill the room. It is thumping, rhythmic, and perfectly in tune with everything. I notice the shaman is chanting to the beat of my heart. This is strange. It's distracting me from the tunnels. She seems to be touching my heart. This is not possible. I feel like she knows me, that she's here with me—but we just met. She cannot know me. She cannot be here with me. I don't know what's going on, but I need to know. I open my eyes, and I'm back in the room. The shaman is playing her drum.

Her drum is my heartbeat. My heartbeat is her drum. She says her drum is the earth. The earth and my heart are one.

She asks me where I've been. I tell her about the tunnels and the colors, and that I was flying, and that it was so very incredible. I tell her that I never wanted to leave that place. She says that she knew that, and that's why she started playing the drum. She brought me back. She played the drum for me.

I've never experienced anything like this before. I am never going to be the same. I feel a certain love I've not felt before. I feel cared for. I feel somehow connected to a part of something very great.

I can't really say if what I experienced was real or imagined. It seemed so real. If it was all just imagined, then the mind is more amazing than I ever could have thought. If there was anything real about it, then this life is more amazing than I ever could have imagined. Ayahuasca is definitely not just some hallucinogenic drug. Ayahuasca just changed my life.

My meditation is now my deepest trance. My dance is now my deepest dance. My spirit meditates with those who choose. My spirit dances with all in the room. I can see so much now, but the world has become quite an unusual place.

CHAPTER 61
THE TRUTH

I JUST WATCHED a car come barreling down a hill where there was an accident waiting at the bottom. The car slammed on its brakes, it skidded, it spun sideways, it spun backwards, it skidded past the accident, it spun sideways again, and it straightened back out. The driver exulted with his arms in the air, the passengers cheered, and then the car sped off down the road. The people involved in the accident and the police on the scene just stood there with their mouths agape, frozen in fear, too shocked to move. They all probably would have died if the car had actually hit them. I sat in my car shaking my head in amazement. What a spectacular event I had just witnessed! I actually wished I had been in the car that skidded; the people in that car have some story to tell. It was no illusion that they were having a very good day.

The illusion lies in not seeing that this world is nothing more than a shell, and that we place our trust in a painted, carved, and decorated hollow space that we believe will support us. We believe that this is the existence we're meant for. Jump up and down a few times. You might break through the shell, and there will be a sudden drop, and it's all so fragile, and the ground is up, and the sky is down, and all the shapes are backwards, and everything is in pieces. I don't know where my head is now, and I don't know where my feet are. I'm falling—or I'm flying. This is terrifying—or it's ecstatic. I might be at the bottom of the hill, or I might be at the top of the hill. My mouth might be agape with a stifled scream, or my mouth might be projecting an ecstatic cheer. I may miraculously spin around death, or I'll be frozen in the middle of the road, but I don't know when I made these choices. I can only see where I am. I do believe there is something deliberate going on, though. I can decide if it's a good idea to jump up and down. I might break through, or I might not break through. But I'm going to go in some direction.

When coming over a hill, you know you're moving toward the bottom of the hill, and you know that something's going to be at the bottom of the hill, but you continue to drive. Perhaps you like to drive fast with your friends in the car. This is not a prescribed way to behave. I have driven a car that skidded. You bear down face-first, shatter everything, never hit anything, and then cheer that you're still alive. This is the truth. I want to live my life exulting with my arms in the air. I want *everyone* to live their lives exulting with their arms in the air. It's no longer about the direction that we're heading. The greatest part of spiritual practice can be that moment when you don't know where you're going. I am told that this is just a part of the practice, and that practice will not replace the realities of life. But when you say this, I don't believe you.

I believe in what's become obvious to me. The storm is approaching, the dragon bellows, the landslide's encroaching, and the thunder echoes. I am about to know what I need to know. It's time to crush the crayon that I've used to make up my face. I will never be able to look at this reflection again. I'm going to wake up tomorrow, and I don't know how I'll comb my hair. I've accomplished a lot. I've made it impossible to present myself the way that I have always presented myself. I could be terrified, or I could be ecstatic. Instead, I stare into what is now the unknown. It is here that there is deliverance brought about by practice. It is when I am here that I know the truth.

CHAPTER 62

RELINQUISHMENT

I SEE THAT there is still more for me to do. There are still things that are hurting me; they have not gone away. I cannot make these things go away. I can experience what seems like everything, but I am still too influenced by the effects of the world. I think we all know that this is how it is, but I've come to believe that there can be complete freedom from suffering. It is difficult to experience complete freedom from suffering while still being influenced by the effects of the world.

Take a look at the world. A human being experiences all the comfortable and uncomfortable situations of the world. We were born as human beings, and we will continue to live as human beings until we die. Comfortable and uncomfortable situations will always be a possibility for us. If we are to realize complete freedom from suffering, there's got to be something more for us than what we were born into.

I believe that spiritual practice has led me in this direction. After years of dedication, refinement, movement, and exploration, I've come to see my body as nothing more than a group of elements that have combined in a complex and wonderful fashion. I interact with and experience life using the five senses and the mind. I have free will and the ability to direct my thoughts in different directions. This is what I am, and it's perfectly suited to carry me where I need to go, but there is more. There is a traditional Buddhist story I was once told called "The Turtle and the Fish" that tells us what more there is.

There once was a pond, and in it lived a turtle and some fish. One day as the turtle was swimming with the fish, he decided that he would go up on land to take a walk. So, the turtle climbed up on land and took a walk. A short while later, he came back to the pond and started swimming with the fish again.

The fish wondered where he had gone. They asked him, "Where did you go?" The turtle told them that he had gone up on land to take a walk. "Take a walk on land?" the fish asked. "What is that?" The turtle told them it would be pretty hard for him to explain.

"Please try. We want to know." "I don't believe that I can." The fish were confused. They decided to ask some questions.

"Well, is it all wet up on land?" asked the fish.

"It's not all wet," said the turtle.

"Do you float around on land?" asked the fish.

"No, you don't float around," said the turtle.

"Do you use your flippers to propel yourself up, down, and sideways when you're up on land?" asked the fish.

"No, you don't do that either," said the turtle. "This land is a very mysterious place," said the fish. "We don't understand." "I know. I didn't think you would understand," said the turtle.

We can only fully understand what we are when what we are can be expressed in our lives. It is this experience that changes us. When the circumstances and the solutions to the circumstances are no longer necessary, the time will come. The path will be followed, and there is little else to do. Then the beauty that has always been here appears. It will become possible to emerge from the depths, walk together, and discuss the flowers. They are so pretty.

CHAPTER 63

PEACE

THE PEACE AT this time is still somewhere inside. This peace can become apparent, though. One experiences clarity, and the forces underlying what needs to be done become evident. I feel what haunts me, pursue that which takes the unfamiliar away, and do it with conviction.

Initially, I needed to exercise restraint to achieve my goals, but that restraint turned to choice, and that choice became a way of life. It was no longer a choice when I no longer needed to decide what to do. Things once misunderstood have become known. See how this journey has been. Everything that has brought me to where I am has already been written. One only needs to look, and my methods are obvious. My heart is on the paper.

See where I've been confused along the way. I've come to know the world and what has confused me, but I've been engaged with what confuses me, and once I'm engaged, it's hard to be any other way.

Spiritual practice presents its own version of things. In the midst of extremes and seemingly unflinching attachment, there could be calm. There's an existence that can penetrate what is seen, heard, touched, tasted, smelled, and thought. It becomes possible to redefine what is real. This need not be hard to believe. In this age of science and knowledge, mysteries can still be found that amaze. This is exciting. Look for the mysteries, and live in the mysteries. It's within these mysteries that liberation awaits.

A mystery inside of you. A mystery inside of me. A mystery inside every single person. Imagine what may be inside. Count to one, then let go of one. Count to two, then let go of two. Count to three, then let go of three. Stop imagining; we're already doing it.

CHAPTER 64

THOUGHTS

IMAGINATION PERSISTS, THOUGH. I can't stop thinking about it, but there is a reason. The mind I was once so familiar with is growing quiet, and the quieting mind will spread its embers throughout a being. It can be fascinating to watch the mind's fight for survival. It's okay to be fascinated when it's yourself that you're fascinated with. The hooks will eventually be removed with ease. It's exactly what needs to be done. I'm in the process of dismantling a personality. I'm in the process of freeing the mind.

I need to know what to look for. I will be turning to the mind to accomplish great things. This mind changes with changing circumstances, though. It's trying to manage constant variation. It's not insulated from what is being felt. Here is what I see when I look. The mind is chasing a solution, and it's no wonder that the solution needs to be chased, since the solution comes from the world.

It's ironic that the world is making available what is needed for us to relinquish the world. We have something to let go of. This is backwards. We're looking for something to hang onto. We'll never find something to hang onto, though; everything's impermanent. Perhaps it is we who are backwards. I'm ecstatic. Everything that I see myself to be comes entirely from this mind, and none of it is real.

Whenever I think that something is secure, it is just the mind. Whenever I think that something is not secure, it is just the mind. Whenever I think that something is pleasant, unpleasant, or neither pleasant nor unpleasant, it is just the mind. I'm taking this someplace. We can change the mind, but we can't change anything else, because the conditions for anything else arising have already happened. The conditions for the arising of the mind are happening right now.

Look down at the body. Everything that happens with the mind relies upon the body. Smack your thigh, feel it, and then think about it. Or maybe don't feel it, and don't think about it. What a strange use of time.

One day, I was watching my mind spin off, and I just let it go. It was following a feeling. I wasn't interested. Then the mind looked back and wondered where its thoughts were. It craved nourishment. It was starving. It seemed like it was dying. I was so scared. I felt that this mind could not die, or I would die too. I saw the body breathing, healthy, and capable. This mind isn't going to die. I smacked my thigh, and I laughed. Unenlightened people are often irrational. There's nothing wrong with it. I just needed to admit that. I watched my mind spin off again, and I let it go. A peaceful person will not be born.

I don't always like that I was born. I recently caught the flu. The flu is such an unusual state to be in. I could barely get out of bed, I was almost always cold, I hardly ate, I was really achy, and I slept a lot. I saw it coming on; I've had the flu before. I thought, *Oh no, I think I'm getting the flu!* I took vitamin C, oregano oil, and elderberry, and drank lots of water and tea, but it was too late. It got me. I had to ride it out for about a week. This is typical.

Then it was gone. I jumped out of bed one day, went to work, danced in the street, and I was all better. The best way to deal with the flu is to not ever get the flu.

One learns much from life. I see what happens once something gets started. The peaceful or unpeaceful states will end when they end. There are things I can do that will sustain peace, and there are things I can do that will destroy peace. I would like to define the process.

I am here right now, I am aging, and I am going to die someday. There's nothing that can stop this. So much has been accomplished, and so much has yet to be accomplished. When I am happy, content, and feel fulfilled, then perhaps the journey has made it to a good place. When I am unhappy, discontent, and unfulfilled, then perhaps the striving is still unwinding. See what determines every outcome. I see what brought me here.

It's just the events of life playing out. Things change from good to bad, and from bad to good, and not in any particular order. I'm going to experience the effects of changes. I often think that I'm ready to handle what's going to happen. I've lived for a long time. Still, I don't know for sure. Even the Buddha had a bad back. My back is currently okay, but everything that's a part of this body is eventually going to turn to dust. The only way that something will not to turn to dust is if it never arises from dust in the first place.

I've actually never seen dust do anything special. It will blow around my room when I don't clean it. I do like the idea of an exploding universe of dust coming together to form planets, suns, moons, and people, though. It's probably more than just an idea. My ideas can be pretty convincing. My ideas can sometimes be right.

I picture how the future will be, and this changes how the future will be. The future is always affected by the present moment. This instills a sense of responsibility in me. If I think about this, I might just do nothing. I like the way things are right now. Sometimes I don't like the way things are. However, I still may do nothing. At least there's still something inside. I have a lot of things inside.

I remember when I watched a friend of mine turn a corner and get hit in the face with a blisteringly fast snowball. It was me; I threw the snowball. It was a real screamer. If we had been in outer space, it would have been a comet. My team won that snowball fight. We had a great time. I'll never forget it. There's an interesting nature to what stays with me.

Perhaps it's because I'm a writer. I continually search for things to write about. I toss around ideas over and over in my mind. I'll be in a good mood or a bad mood depending on what I find in there. It's amazing to see the power that my thoughts could have. How I treat other people, how I treat myself, how I sleep, how I eat, and how the next moment is going to be for me can be dependent upon just a few words. It's about the feeling, and feelings are powerful.

At one point, there was a person in my life who didn't make me feel good. It seemed like I was always doing something wrong in their eyes. Sometimes I wasn't even sure what it was. I thought I was trying to have a conversation. I thought I was expressing an opinion. I wouldn't mean any harm, and yet harm would occur. I often grew sad because of this. It eventually became difficult enough that I just walked away.

This is freedom. There was nothing for me to be aggravated about anymore. I just needed to remove my life from a situation. It took some time for me to see it. Solutions are pretty easy once they're implemented.

My neighbor then got on my nerves. We were very different from each other. There were parts of my life that required a significant amount of attention. If things didn't happen the way they were supposed to, a lot could go wrong. I took this very seriously. He was much calmer about things. I think that if I had told him my hair was on fire, he would've said, "All right, Mike, just put it out." But it's not always that easy.

Look at my claim to freedom. Freedom from one place delivered me to another place. I wonder how much blame will be handed out before I die. We come in contact with a lot of things before we die. I know that I search for the things that bring me happiness. I'll jump into a waterfall, have lunch with thirty people, go to a party, and bleach my hair. We'll ride our bikes to the beach, swim with the dolphins, take our suits off, and learn to stay warm in a pile of four. Let's get crazy! Let's throw a boomerang that has no bend, run down a mountain even though we can't stand, and dance to the music when there is no band. The bar is set to its high mark.

I know what's going on, though. No matter how good things are, everything else is still happening. Things are living and dying right in front of me. Everything is changing, and I can't stop this. Everything is going to live and die the way it was meant to. We're in touch, and then we're not. We're together, and then we're not. I'm always paying attention to things like this. The mind is a part of things like this.

I've learned that when the mind does well, the body does well. It's my job to find out how much history is needed to make it all come true. I need to be patient. Just picture the task at hand. The conditioning started when time itself started. People have the capacity for boundless good, but the right choices still have to be made.

So, I dig into what's within. There's an energy in there that drives me. I don't want to have to stop or start the energy. I only want what drives me to be expressed. This is the way to be genuine, but it might not look pretty.

When I used to run the streets, I did things that were not pretty. I was being genuine in service of a craving that told me I needed more. I felt like I had no choice. There was a purity to it all. Having to make a decision to survive each day is a simple decision to make. But the rest of life fell apart in the wake of my selfishness.

Those brilliant ideas seemed to surface from nowhere, but ideas do have their origins, and my actions based on my ideas do have their consequences. I'm a boiling pot of water filling the room with steam. I want people to come see me, and I want their stay to be pleasant. I'm now wary of what's in the pot on the stove. The room is going to hold the essence of what I'm doing.

I'm going to tell you more. The unwise being knows not where to turn; the being who is wise turns to what is learned. You could say that I'm fortunate. I know that I can't do anything about the way that things have been, but we all must live with what we've become.

CHAPTER 65

COCOON

IT'S AS IF I'm a man in a cocoon. Only now can I see it. It's hard to see when you're contained within a shell. It's the best explanation I have for what's gone on with me, though. Look at some of the things that I do.

I watch movies about heroes. I like the ones that are suspenseful and action-filled. The main character seems unfit to take on some dangerous challenge, but in the movie, there is a dangerous challenge, and the character takes it on anyway.

The person is falling, but throws a rope out at the last minute; they almost drown, but grab a tank of air; they're chased by bandits, but the bandits are no match; they're on a perilous journey, but remarkably, they get there. It's unmistakable, the impossible that happens.

I experience doubt along the way. It wouldn't be much of a movie if there wasn't doubt. The situations that people get themselves into can scare me. Once on the other side, though, everything is clear again. It's not the time to stop.

The path extends forward, and there's another corner to turn, another cliff to fall off of, another flood of concern. The bandits will try to steal from you; it's just what the bandits do.

The audience watches with bated breath, clutching and holding each other. I love the crowd, and the popcorn, and the cherry soda. I'm not here alone. The thrill is felt by all. There is the booming sound, the flashing lights, the rush of applause, and then the grand ending. The hero triumphs, sips a drink, and walks off, ready for the next adventure. I feel as if I could do anything now. I am so inspired.

I sit back in my chair and reflect on my life. I too have been confronted with danger, but it's been different for me. It's like I've been in a cocoon. I could feel the danger, but am mainly a spectator. I am amazed that I was never discovered, but am grateful that I can still be inspired.

It's the inspiration that has kept me striving. It's the danger that has kept my heart pumping. It's only when wisdom arises that I learn it's time for me to go.

I wish I had only instincts, because then I would just fly away. I am more than just instincts, though. I am a being of the mind, and the mind can go in many directions. I have developed compassion for others, and I apply compassion to myself. This is my mind today. It's what keeps me alive, but I still envy the heroes. They're the ones who are truly brave.

Allow me to explain my version of bravery. Many times I've been falling, but the rope was already there; many times I've been drowning, but was given that breath of air; many times I ran from bandits, but my race I never shared. I could be seen as brave. I've been confronted with challenges and met with adversity, and have often emerged with only a bruise. I didn't set that rope up, though; I don't produce the air; I easily ran the race I won; the others weren't there. The seclusion of my life has allowed me to be brave.

It's a cocoon. It's a life inside of a shell. Yes, I should've been dead, I should've been broken, I should've lost my mind, but instead, I'm in the midst of a transformation. I just don't know what I'm transforming into. You know what it's been like. I relish a practice that has no goal, but it's kept my demons at bay.

Sometimes I can still see these demons. They're familiar. They came in the door that I tried to keep closed, they picked on me whenever they chose, and they kissed the girl who I once loved the most. I can feel them today when they shake my bed. They are the same as they have always been. However, I am not the same. I know that I have the ability to grow wings, and people with wings fly with the spirit.

The day will soon come when the demons won't know what to do. I am going to rise above them, see them for what they are, look back at where I just was, and bid them good-bye. Tired old demons don't know how to fly. "You will no longer find me," I will say, "there is someplace else for me to be." I think I'm ready.

The cocoon that I have lived in is about to break open; the protections I've relied on will become no more; the rumors that the light won't find its way in are about to lose their final score.

Look at what's happening. I can see what's happening. I see how my life has been. There's been an amazing world all around me, and I've not lived in it the way that most people do.

Instead, I look down and see that there's a broken shell. I can stand, I can stretch, and I can unfurl my wings. All that I have done has nourished these wings. It has shattered this shell. You would think that this would be the greatest moment of my life. It is enlightening to write about, but life has its surprises.

CALIFORNIA

CHAPTER 66
THE VISION

EVERYTHING SEEMS TO be right where I want it to be now. My practice is penetrative, and it is consistent. I dance regularly and have a great group of dancer friends. My job is secure, and it is fulfilling. My financial situation is good, my living arrangements are good, my health is good, and I am feeling good … but my boss just called me. They want to promote me; they want me to become a boss. It sounds great! It offers more money, more security, and less people above me at work telling me what to do. I am going to need to move to California, though; I am going to have to leave New York City. This is not an easy decision to make. I've established a happy life here in New York City, but as my friend once told me, "You take you with you."

If I move to California, I'm going to take me with me. I am an established Buddhist practitioner, I am a dancer, I am a seeker, and I am a seer. I've accomplished great things in my life. I do things now that I never thought I would do.

I experience things that I never thought I would experience. There's no reason for me not to take the opportunity being presented to me. I've changed the way I am living where I live. I can do whatever I want anywhere I go.

I'm moving to California, and something unexpected just happened. I was walking to go get dinner. It was a pleasant cool night out tonight. I had my sweatshirt on, and I was enjoying it. It reminded me of the nights when I used to walk everywhere. It's the kind of memory that people like to tell stories about—those happy carefree days of old. Then there was this pain. It was in my heart, it was in my head, it was all around me. I saw people staring down at me, chastising me and berating me, and I felt small and terrified. I didn't know what was going on. I didn't know why this was happening to me. I didn't know why I was being treated the way I was being treated. I didn't do anything bad; I'm just being me. I know that I might act a little strange once in a while, but there's nothing wrong with that. Only apparently, there is something wrong with that. At least, that's what I was always told. This is what my carefree days of old were like.

I kept walking, but the feeling only intensified. I was shaking. I know now to breathe. I know to count my steps. Soon I would be at the supermarket, staring at the salad bar. I would make myself a salad and pick out a dessert and something to drink. I was just a grown man going to get some dinner. No, I wasn't; I felt like a child on the outskirts in front of a salad bar. I had just had a vision of the traumatized child that is still inside me.

The idea of leaving New York is having an effect on me that I didn't anticipate. I didn't realize how much I really liked my friends, the nice place that I live, the job I have, and the routine I've established. Now that it's all about to change, I can see how much those things have propped me up and sustained me. I have constructed a level of security from something that I thought was anything but that.

This is still a mind that can suffer. My spiritual practice has shown me a lot of things, has brought me a lot of joy, and has brought about seemingly impossible changes in who I am, how I feel, and how I act. But I see now that my spiritual practice, as impossible and illogical as I believe it all to be, is still just close to the surface. A ripple in its workings has brought me to a panic. I am committed to moving, though. I am all set to go to California, and as soon as I move, I have a plan: I'm going to go dancing.

CHAPTER 67

LOSS

DANCING IN CALIFORNIA does not work for me. It doesn't bring me to that magical place that dancing in New York brought me to. It's not that dancing is bad in California; there are 5Rhythms classes, but they are not the same. I don't want to dance here.

Meditation in California is not working for me. It doesn't bring me to that deep, serene place that meditation in New York brought me to. It's not that meditation doesn't exist in California, it just feels different. I don't want to meditate here.

I'm sure there's plenty of ayahuasca in California, but I don't want to take the time to look for it. I loved the ayahuasca ceremony I did in New Jersey. I loved the shaman that conducted it. I don't want to search for another; I don't know that I could find what I would be looking for.

I've lost my motivation. I would not have thought that was possible. I thought I was rooted in the unknown, but now I see just how fragile my peace really is. My successful emergence from my cocoon was dependent on the environment I was emerging into, and now that I live in California, the environment that I'm emerging into here looks just like a cave.

CHAPTER 68

THE SHADOWS

I AM LOOKING out at this beautiful life all around me, but this beautiful life may not even exist. The shadows of a cave obscure what I see. I can create pictures on the walls, but the pictures are only made of ash, or dye, or mere scratches. You can't talk to a scratch on the wall. It doesn't answer your questions.

The sun shines outside of my cave. The sunshine is certainly real. I know, I see it, but I retreat. I live in the shadows. I sleep and eat in the shadows. I tell you that I go home to my beautiful house and a steak dinner cooked on the barbecue, but it's really just a cave to me. I wish I could just blow up the whole mountain. Then the cave would have no place to be a hole in. The rock walls would be gone.

Instead, I look around at the rock walls. I see the scratches that I have created here. There's the Buddhism; those magical words are meticulously recorded. There are the beautiful dancers; the beautiful dancers are perfectly drawn. There's the ayahuasca; if I look hard enough, I can actually see the spinning, wonderfully colorful geometry of a most spectacular mind.

I've always reveled in this type of creativity. There's sheer beauty in the simplicity. The mystical shapes, the abstract beings, the sun, and the moon all have their spirit, but now I cry when I look. I can see where I am. In one sense, there's so much awe and joy, but in another sense, there's the pain that is still with me. It's the pain that has always pushed me, though. The more I hurt, the more I strive. I will study further, meditate deeper, dance harder, and then write it all down. Perhaps every creation in the world comes from a place like this. This seemingly eternal human condition just might be what built our bridges, painted our paintings, and wrote our books.

People will say that this is how it's supposed to be, that life is all about the challenge. We just need to find the right space, stake our claim, and then bathe in the cool water, but this can be awful or wonderful. I know how awful or wonderful it can be. The cravings for existence and inclusion once led me to the riskiest places, but now I'm living in California, in a safe place, with a good job. I sometimes wish I had started a family, joined a dart league, and saved money for the future, but that's not how it's been for me. Many people probably find it easy to live their lives. Their trauma, their influences, their lives went a certain way. Everybody's life goes a certain way.

My life went the way of dedicated spiritual practice. My life has become the result of my practice, but now my practice looks like a drawing on a cave wall. This is quite a shock. I feel as if I'm slapping all the people that I have come to know and love in the face. The Buddhists and the dancers probably don't know. My ayahuasca shaman is an amazing friend, with amazing abilities, and yet she now just looks like a drawing on a cave wall. This is how I perceive it all to be, yet I still feel there must be a purpose.

Maybe it's that in a few thousand years, an explorer is going to find my cave. This person might make sketches of what they've found. People will marvel at the details and wonder what it all means. They'll contemplate the ancient being who once created such amazing works. They might realize that human beings ancient and current all share the same mind, the same spirit, and the same will to live and be happy—but this doesn't do me any good right now.

This is a place without sunshine. I think I might just need to get used to the world being this way for me. My existence has become one of carefully constructed protection. My life has been spent working hard, just trying to ease my pain. It's amazing that there is still gloom after there's been so much work. I wonder if anyone else can see inside. Just try staring into my eyes. You don't know what's in here, and I'm confused, but you're not a mind reader. You can only look at the gloss that looks back at you. I don't know that you can't see me. It should be no surprise that I'm confused. Unless I express what's behind these eyes, there will always just be a vacant stare. I don't know that I can express anything; I live in a cave.

Sometimes I stand at the entrance because it's where I like to stand, and you walk by again. You do this all the time. You approach me and offer to share your blanket with me. I agree, and I sit with you, and we talk about all the different things, and you listen. I feel the warmth on my face, and so I look up. It's the sun. I can feel the sun. I look into your eyes, and I want to get to know you.

I believe that I have to do something.

CHAPTER 69
SURFING

I JUST WENT out and bought a surfboard and a wetsuit. I may not want to dance, meditate, or go on hallucinogenic journeys while I'm in California, but I can surf. I'm going to take whatever is going on with me and give it to the Pacific Ocean.

I've always loved the ocean. Growing up on the East Coast offered me plenty of opportunities to go to the beach. I remember walking on the boardwalk, swimming in the waves, riding the carnival rides, and enjoying all the great beach food. It was a long time ago; it was the Jersey shore of the seventies and eighties. I was almost always comfortable down at the beach.

Now I'm down at the Pacific Ocean. I'm at one of the great beaches off the Southern California coast. It's one of the more popular attractions that California has to offer people. If I'm going to live in a cave, it may as well be a beach. I can be comfortable here too.

There is no boardwalk, though. There are no carnival rides. This is not a time from long ago. I'm done with those drunken times. I did buy a wetsuit and a surfboard, though. Those surfers look like they can fly.

I'd never seen a surfer before—men and women dressed all in black, paddling out through the waves just to turn around and glide back to the shore. It looks so magical. It looks like so much fun. I need something fun to do.

I just got thrown down. This rugged Pacific Ocean of the West is not the calm Atlantic of the East. My surfboard is a plank. I'm standing in a churning ocean with an eight-foot plank in my hands. This is crazy. I can't even begin to lie down on this thing. I keep falling off. The waves never stop. This is so hard. I am so tired. I need to breathe. I need to come back another day.

I'm back. Take it slow. The ocean is a bit calmer today. I just need to learn to lay down on my board without falling off. This day's work is over.

The next day's and the next day's work is over; I can lay down on a surfboard.

I need to learn how to paddle. I'm going to need to paddle this way and that if I'm ever going to ride a wave. It is so tiring, paddling this way and that. I can paddle here, and rest, and try not to roll off. I can paddle there, and rest, and try not to roll off. This is what surfing is like for me. It's not gliding around on a wave; it's flailing. I'm learning to flail. It's amazing when I am unhappy with things how I will try and do just one thing. Paddle hard and try not to cringe, paddle hard before the waves begin, paddle hard with just the right spin, and paddle on my belly until I ride the wave in.

This is how I'm learning to surf: months spent in white water, occasionally riding a wave in on my belly. I am training my body and my mind for what's about to come. There's a lot of soreness. I spend many days just lying on the couch nursing a hurt neck, knee, shoulder, chest, or back. If I'm going to surf, I'm going to have to earn it.

The afternoon is here. I am on my belly, the wave is pushing me, everything feels stable, time is standing still, and I am standing up on my board. For a mere few seconds, I cruise a blend of white water, rumble, and mush until I fall off. It is one of the coolest feelings I've ever felt. It seems like I am the clumsiest, most awkward surfer on the beach, but I am so thrilled with what I just did.

Everything is taking off now. After about a year of flapping around, I can ride a white-water wave. I hang in the shallows, a wave comes in, I jump on my board, the wave pushes, and I stand up. Over and over it occurs, but this is not the goal. To paddle out into the deep just to sit and wait with all the surfers who know what they're doing is the goal. To see a big, beautiful wave come in, paddle right along with it, pop up, cruise down its face, and ride like the wind is the goal, but that can be a terrifying idea.

I once paddled out into the deep water and looked back toward the shore. The shore was pretty far away. This is not a place that a human being should be just sitting on a board. A wave rolled in, and I wasn't ready. It threw me from my board, and just like that, I was tumbling head over heels underwater, unable to surface. I panicked, just wanting to stand on the friendly beach again. Standing on the beach, I survived. One of the best lessons learned while surfing is that you will survive. Time and again, I've paddled out into the deep water, and I've survived. Sooner or later, I'm going to do more than just survive.

I paddled out again into the deep water and looked back toward the shore. The view has become so beautiful from here. I am so lucky to be out here just sitting on a board. A wave is rolling in, I am paddling right along, the wave is pushing me, and I am up, and I am screaming down the face of the wave, I am gliding, I am surfing. I can't believe what just happened! I'm now standing on the friendly beach, panting. The adrenaline is so high. That was one of the greatest feelings of my entire life. I surfed!

Now I wake up early, as I have always done. I drink tea, I read a little, I eat an energy bar, and I head to the beach to go surfing. It's been two years since I first stepped into the Pacific Ocean with a board in my hands. So much has changed since then. I now sit out back with all the other surfers, waiting for a wave. "Sitting out back" is a surfing term for waiting out in the deep water for a wave to come in. I know things like this now; I've become a Southern California surfer.

We wait for the waves, look around at each other, pick just the right wave at the right time, execute all the right moves, and glide in to shore. Over and over this goes on. I can describe what we do, but I cannot describe how it makes any of us feel. A surfer once said to me, "It's not what it looks like," and this is true.

CHAPTER 70
METAMORPHOSIS

THE BUDDHA ACTUALLY taught it to me, the dancers always danced it with me, and the shaman gleefully sang it for me. Things are not what they look like. The feelings, the emotions, and the experiences happen in that moment, and then there is the truth. I sit with a meditator, dance with a dancer, journey with a shaman, and I surf with the surfers. It's here, and then it's gone—but a moment could change everything.

When I'm sitting on my surfboard there's no time for thought, for worry, or for speculation. There's just the ocean, and there's the wave. If I'm going to ride that wave, it's all there can be. The anxiety, the childhood trauma, my long illustrious past can all haunt me as I sit and wait. The wave comes, and I'm sent tumbling to the bottom. The pain and the fear are great agitators, but the body and the mind know how to heal themselves. After years of practice, I no longer tumble. I feel confident in what I've become.

I'm currently out on my board in water deep enough to drown me, just waiting for my ideal wave, and it calms me, connects me, gives me time to reflect and settle the mind and body. I'm seeing my wave arrive, and it enthralls me, motivates me, and spurs me into action. I catch that wave, and it is crazy, exciting, uncertain, but it's what I do. I glide down the face of the beautiful wave, and it is fun, it's like flying, it's ecstatic. Finally, I step off at the end, and it is amazing, fulfilling, a goal accomplished, a transformation realized. We can be the enigmatic and beautiful people who end up here.

CHAPTER 71
DWELLING

RIGHT NOW I'M looking at my surroundings. I'm sitting in a house, and it's no longer a cave, and I realize everything. Everything that's around me was once just a thought, an idea. Someone had an idea for this house that I live in, this chair that I'm sitting on, this table that I'm writing on, and this coffee that I'm drinking. I feel as if all the world that has been created by human hands is actually just a vast collection of ideas that have turned into something. Look at what we have done!

I sometimes wonder if it's really working. Perhaps you are comfortable, happy, and healthy, and your neighbors are comfortable, happy, and healthy, but there are those of us who are not. You cannot give me your paycheck, though, or you will not eat. You must eat, so therefore, I will starve. This is what we have created. I see it, I just came out of a cave. I've stepped away from where I once was, so therefore I can see.

I too am just like this house, this chair, this table, and this cup of coffee. I am a collection of ideas that have turned into something. If we take away all that makes up the houses, chairs, tables, and coffee, I see what's left. The trees and the grass will appear in their place, and they are perfect just as they are. The trees and the grass will heal this world. If I take away that which makes up what I am, I see what's left. Emptiness will appear in my place, and I am perfect just as I am. The truth will heal this being.

That which makes up our world is here no matter what, though. This is our karma, but I can turn to the grass and the trees, as they love to be seen. That which makes up what I am is not here no matter what, though. This is my karma. I can also turn to this truth, as it too loves to be seen.

We are nature, but fleeting, and strive to be alive. We appear as a result. I embrace this belief, and then I am able embrace everything and everyone. The years of stripping away the delusion left me vacant, clear, and spacious, until there was only one thing left to do.

CHAPTER 72
LA WOMAN

I MOVED INTO this house with someone. It is you who used to walk by—an LA woman, just like Jim Morrison used to sing about. This is new to me, and I have some things to learn. I do know that this life I'm living is not meant to be lived in isolation. However, I still admire the wanderers, the solitary sage, and the oracle on the mountaintop. People search these great beings out. No one comes searching for me, though, and now I see that no one has to.

I enjoy meals with you, and love, and we watch our shows on the big TV. I ride my bike with you, and we dance, and we squint our eyes when we're at the beach. You are my partner, my best friend. You're intimate with me, and it addresses our needs. We don't always get along, but we always get along again. We're together all the time, but still, there's time with my pen. We cuddle close, just the two of us, then meddle alone when we know that we must. This is my life today. I want to share what I am, and because I'm now not alone, I know that I can.

I don't need to be the oracle on the mountaintop. I only need to be a part of this life that I now live. There is isolation, and then there's not. There is practice, but then it stops. There is wonder, but then you give what you've got. I still have my theories, my striving, my progress, and my will for perfection. But when we're together, you are my theories, my striving, my progress, and my will for perfection, and I enjoy that you are. It's okay for me to enjoy, for when I enjoy, I see that you enjoy too. Perhaps all the changes that I've made, the wonder that exists, and the peace that I feel today have come down to living just this way.

You welcomed me in, every day we begin, and I don't look for the end, because when we spin, we spin together. I've sometimes wondered if this is where I would end up, and now that I am here, I see that this is exactly where I want to be.

It's still not always easy. Still I have to try. I seem to have to try with everything, but I remember something. The Buddha would know what I should do now. He spoke of a divine way to exist. I've tried to understand the divine for years, but it always seemed to elude me. I've heard friends talk about the divine, I've been to classes on the divine, I've read about the divine, and now I'm going to try and live in the divine.

I'm going to quote the Buddha one final time:

One abides pervading one quarter with a mind imbued with loving-kindness, likewise the second, likewise the third, likewise the fourth; so above, below, around, and everywhere, and to all as to oneself, one abides pervading the all-encompassing world with a mind imbued with loving-kindness, abundant, exalted, immeasurable, without hostility and without ill will.

One abides pervading one quarter with a mind imbued with compassion, likewise the second, likewise the third, likewise the fourth; so above, below, around, and everywhere, and to all as to oneself, one abides pervading the all-encompassing world with a mind imbued with compassion, abundant, exalted, immeasurable, without hostility and without ill will.

One abides pervading one quarter with a mind imbued with appreciative joy, likewise the second, likewise the third, likewise the fourth; so above, below, around, and everywhere, and to all as to oneself, one abides pervading the all-encompassing world with a mind imbued with appreciative joy, abundant, exalted, immeasurable, without hostility and without ill will.

One abides pervading one quarter with a mind imbued with equanimity, likewise the second, likewise the third, likewise the fourth; so above, below, around, and everywhere, and to all as to oneself, one abides pervading the all-encompassing world with a mind imbued with equanimity, abundant, exalted, immeasurable, without hostility and without ill will.

I know how I should treat you. I just have to do it. It's true that I have to turn to a teaching to know these things, but I have gratitude that there even is a teaching. I only need to make a choice. Today I am confident that I can be shown the way.

You've taught me that a person deserves to be treated with kindness, so I treat you with kindness. You've confided in me that a person needs compassion when they are hurting, so I show you compassion when you're hurting. You've shared with me that a joyful person likes it when I'm a part of their joy, so I let myself be a part of your joy. You've shown me that a person is never perfect and that sometimes I need to just let things go, so I sometimes just let things go.

It expands from here. The results prove my point. I now get along with those who may be different, I'm a friend to those who may need a friend, I laugh with those who tend to laugh, and I give space to those who would see me descend. I treat myself like never before, I'm good to myself when I have no more. I enjoy myself when the times are good, and I allow myself to be free when I should.

It took so much for me to get to this place. My dilemma occurs when I think of how long it took. I could have done these things such a long time ago. Its better when I don't look back and just let today be today, but when I do look back, perhaps I could see it all in a different way.

CHAPTER 73
DIVINE ABODES

"One is resolved only upon the beautiful."
– The Buddha

I'VE BEEN THE ecstatic winner, and the devastated loser; the one who lives forever, and the one who dies a beggar; the thief of the treasure, and the unknown fortune teller.

There is neither plus nor minus, good nor bad, infinite nor final, happy nor sad. I am not the winner, and I'm not the loser; I don't live forever, and I'm not a beggar. I didn't steal your treasure, and I'm not your fortune teller. We are one and the same because everyone is neither plus nor minus, good nor bad, infinite nor final, happy nor sad. No one is a winner, no one a loser, no one lives forever, but we are all here as beggars, and we didn't steal the treasure, because we are all fortune tellers. This may be hard to understand, or there might be some things about me that you can relate to. You just might be able to identify with this struggle of mine.

Life always seems to be a struggle for me. I think that's obvious by now. Decades of drug addiction, deep

217

commitment to my recovery, Buddhist practice, dancing, surfing, and here I am still writing. It goes on. It shouldn't surprise me that I am again here.

Everything should work in my perfected game, it seems like nothing would need to change, and I can just live where things aren't so strange. But this place goes away sometimes so fast, the perfection I've felt; it never lasts, as the peace yet again does ultimately pass. It's hard to think that this is all for naught, it doesn't make sense that I can't reach what I've sought, surely there's something that I must've caught. Perhaps there is!

I turn to a story that I heard a monk tell a long time ago. It went something like this: "So, when I had been a monk for about twenty years, I was ready to give up. I always thought that becoming a monk was going to give me some great insight, some profound knowledge, and that I was going to feel wonderful all of the time, but that didn't happen. I was disappointed and sad. I felt I had made a bad choice with my life. I decided to go to my teacher to tell him that I was going to quit being a monk.

"I found him sitting quietly. I looked at him and said, 'I'm done with being a monk. I've been at this now for twenty years, and I do everything that a monk in my position is supposed to do. I am now a teacher of monks, a leader in our monastery, but I feel that I am no different than I was when I first became a monk. This practice, this lifestyle, didn't do what I was expecting it to do.' My teacher smiled at me and said, 'Yes, I know. It took me twenty years to realize that too.'"

Wow! I too have been involved in my practice for almost twenty years now, and I can relate to this monk, and I think I know why his teacher smiled. This practice probably won't make me feel wonderful all of the time. I will, however, be able to see what lies within.

I always worked to end my struggles with life, but my struggles only grew. Now I no longer have to work, but just do what I have learned to do. I've been given the chance to love myself. I now can truly love you too.

Please meditate with me, and be immersed in the peace. Dance with me, and let's explode with fire. Come surf with me, and we'll just give it all to something greater than us.

I'm all finished writing now. I once found it difficult to write about the past, and I've found it enlightening to write about the past, but now I'm done writing about the past. Your life is a journey.

ABOUT THE AUTHOR

Michael Janes is an accomplished Buddhist practitioner, dancer, and surfer. He started writing at the age of thirty nine when he was inspired to transcribe The Buddha's teachings. He's been writing now for nearly twenty years and just finished his first book. Michael currently resides in Los Angeles, California.